Contents

Poetry Ir... ...

Poetry Ireland Review 104

Eagarthóir / Editor

Caitríona O'Reilly

© Poetry Ireland Ltd 2011

Poetry Ireland Ltd/Éigse Éireann Teo gratefully acknowledges the assistance of The Arts Council/An Chomhairle Ealaíon and The Arts Council of Northern Ireland.

Poetry Ireland invites individuals and commercial organisations to become Friends of Poetry Ireland. For more details please contact:

Poetry Ireland Friends Scheme
Poetry Ireland
2 Proud's Lane
off St Stephen's Green
Dublin 2
Ireland

or telephone +353 1 4789974; e-mail management@poetryireland.ie

PATRONS:
Joan and Joe McBreen

ISBN: 1-902121-42-2
ISSN: 0332-2998

ASSISTANT EDITOR: Paul Lenehan, with the assistance of Sara Keats, Eoin Loughlin and David Maybury.
DESIGN: Alastair Keady (**www.hexhibit.com**)
Printed in Ireland by **Brunswick Press Ltd** Unit B2 Bluebell Industrial Estate Dublin 12

Editorial

To edit *Poetry Ireland Review* is to be faced with an embarrassment of riches on a daily basis. The journal has an unusually high number of submissions, the majority of which come from Ireland, but many of which are sent from the UK, the United States, and other anglophone and non-anglo-phone countries. The responsibility of selection is ever-present but in the end rarely difficult. Reading through each submission in turn, quality work rapidly reveals itself. It has been my intention throughout my editorship to give each submission a fair shake; however no editorial filter is infallible and there is the unavoidable problem of taste and other unacknowledged or unconscious biases. *PIR*'s revolving editorship saves it from the continuation of such biases and from the inevitable staleness of any single editorial position.

One of the most pleasing aspects of the more recent phase of my tenure has been the sense that poets are still willing and able to write to the moment; that the spirit of Swiftian spleen is not entirely extinguished. It is a difficult task to make poetry relevant in that way, since to increasing numbers it is – entirely correctly – seen as a rather self-indulgent academic game, a preening irrelevance. Then, just when one is about to give up on it completely and stomp off in a huff, someone saves the day by reminding everyone that it is the bounden duty of the artist to be a fully paid up member of the awkward squad. Harry Clifton's speech on the occasion of his election to the Ireland Chair of Poetry was just such a delicious occur-rence, following our former Taoiseach's intimation that poets should do their bit to boost the busted brand image of Ireland plc. After all, we're in this together, aren't we? Shortly thereafter the spat spawned an unfortu-nate article in *The Irish Times* entitled 'Why shouldn't poets do the State some service?', in which Enda O'Doherty seemed to be suggesting that artists, particularly poets, should not bite the hand that feeds them. As if there were a shortage of deferential snouts in that particular trough.

But people are rightly suspicious of poets and poetry. From Plato, who would not permit poets in his Republic, to Marianne Moore's fastidious contempt: 'I, too, dislike it'; multitudes have smelled a rat and been entirely correct in doing so. In no other sphere of human endeavour is there such scope for egotism, self-delusion, intellectual narcissism, immaturity, embarrassment, and excruciating self-exposure. But there are still poets in this country honest, brave and self-aware enough to risk massive pratfalls in witnessing, implicitly or explicitly, how the outrages of our times regis-ter on the moral compass of the individual. It is a tricky business. For many writers, Picasso's comment 'I have not painted the war because I am not the kind of kind of painter who goes out like a photographer for something to depict. ... But I have no doubt that the war is in these paint-ings I have done', is the truest summary of what they are trying to achieve. It has been a privilege and a pleasure reading the fresh work in which this occurs and being reminded on a weekly basis that there are indeed still 'imaginary gardens with real toads in them' to be enjoyed.

Thomas Kinsella

LATE LETTERS OF THOMAS MOORE

Senior and friendly,
self-assured and condescending,
he is preoccupied with many concerns.

The phrases are wiped off, as required,
on the self; an odour of authoritative self
rises off the numerous prominent points.

It is all crass from this point in time.

But it would be idle to expect anything different
from an amiable talent, after a lifetime of acclaim.

Thomas Kinsella

THE GUARDIANS

We cleared away the debris from an inner gate,
and found a number of ancient dried figures
fallen partly asunder beneath the stale shelves.

Our scholar picked up an inscribed fragment
from among them, saying with satisfaction:
– It is in the old language, and clear:

Peace. We are the guardians.
Chosen from among the many
Because we were without immediate value.

Thomas Kinsella

ELDERLY CRAFTSMAN AT HIS BENCH

At my worn workbench, in my bent body,
I am disturbed occasionally by an alien fantasy.
Always the same; the detail surreal and distinct:

a soft arm reaching toward me
out of nowhere,
the fingers closing and opening.

I believe now that it is an appeal
from serious efforts, like my own, reaching
unfulfilled from somewhere in the past,

and have learned to put my work to one side;
to relax; and think my way back
into the depths beyond their origin;

appealing to their source to call them back.
Tell them there is no peace here.
And comfort them on their return.

This restores a serviceable calm,
so that I can attend to my work again.
Hoping there will be a like thoughtfulness
for me and my concerns when the time comes.

Frances-Anne King

CROSSING PATER NOSTER SQUARE

Was it the dead, telephoning
down the wire of the wind,

or the ghost of bells
caught in the stillness

of the bone-lit morning light?
Like the thrum of bees' wings

hums and primes pulsed the air
whitening the light between wind-beats.

Ted McCarthy

KILCLOON
  – for Alan and Liz Monahan

I drain another coffee cup
and look out at the sleet that whips
across the lake, now fierce, now spent.
A kid blows on his hands and shunts
his snake of trolleys between cars,
a down and out returns the stares
of giggling schoolgirls on the mitch.
The country tries to start from scratch
but can't resist the urge to splash:
a final binge before the crash,

we keep an old familiar promise
to spend before it's taken from us.
That nation going down the pan,
greedy, venal, also-ran,
our leaders confident, of course,
with not a whisper of remorse.
I think back to that trip we took,
the midlands' leaden floods, the rooks,
your daughter bringing into song
all we hoped when we were young;

the brand new church's leaking roof –
truth in an optimistic life,
the break no hand or word can fix,
whose healing is the time it takes.
Visiting his grave at last,
your son whose funeral I missed
that week I barely recollect,
I realised the pain I'd blocked
no longer mattered next to yours,
your lives a hymn to what endures,

a promise that we will prevail
in spite of all that bodes us ill –
what Hardy deemed capricious fate
or those absurd and petty states

we trail our heart and conscience through:
such parodies of all we know,
where there's no wholeness, no redemption;
just music's sudden consolation,
the cool joy of a late-March thrush,
the drumroll of a deluge-lash:

strange to find such sustenance
in crumbs of varied happenstance,
light given up for lost renewed
by a blade-slit in a sullen cloud.
The sleet subsides. The coffee's cold.
A woman and a well-wrapped child
sit next to me: the easy gesture,
mild intimacy of boy and mother
teasing over Christmas lists,
are all I need to know exists.

D Nurske

VERACRUZ

In that mirror, the lovers watched themselves
undress cautiously, like musicians tuning,
then fuck and sleep arm in arm. When they woke,
the sheen glittered with a cloud of breath
in which they wrote their names with a plus sign
as if they were a sum. They touched Aldebaran.
At dawn they could no longer divide each other
into good and evil – they were too tired.
When they left, the glint was dulled
with a scrim of dust; that city is huge
and the mills grind all night.

They said goodbye to their reflections
blurred like gods, and their faces answered
so long, sorry to part but delighted to remain
safe in happiness, in the pupil of the eye.

John White

CREPUSCULE

At evening tide
the lesser being gravitates
downwards. Mussels, lids pulled bible-tight,

grow dim in Aristotle's
elemental swirl or get sloshed
up, as starfish do, lugged round by toddlers

in bright buckets,
pet-like, slicing the spiny
under-skin, the wrenched off limb that replicates

itself (a star turn,
bright as a buckle) – all this
is unwished, gives rise to taciturn

demeanour. Mute,
at vesper-bell its hymn
is a slow, determined beat that swells the gut.

Vascular stuff,
hydraulic pressure's
what induces us, not head, or mouth:

humped over prey
this stomach can invert.
Though not the heart, which is too heavy.

Howard Wright

STAMPING GROUND

More hidden than seen. More generous than mean.
Less field than park. Less light than dark.

More stylist than barber. More station than harbour.
Less cold than warm. Less snake oil than charm.

More up than down. More country than town.
Less markets than malls. Less barricades than walls.

More telly than radio. More satellite than video.
Less Parton than Presley. Less Calvin than Wesley.

More linen than cotton. More innocent than rotten.
Less petrol than diesel. Less rose than teasel.

More fat than thin. More stout than gin.
Less belisha than zebra. Less knickers than bra.

More forgetful than forgiving. More limbo than heaven.
Less ribbon than nuclear. Less history than fear.

Howard Wright

PERISH THE THOUGHT

The menstrual hour-glass of Ingrid Bergman has a celadon purity.
'The Minstrel of Ardglass' by Ingmar Bergman is a Carleton parody.

Daniel Hardisty

BRIDE

If I were to leave unannounced,
the band still playing in the wooded glade,
the drinks on tables and the bar wide open:

you're the one I'd take my cue from.
The way you slipped out the side door,
not even collecting your coat,

walking away from the marquee in winter
into the cold nut-scented air,
the dresses with their backs to you,

and the bright-sided tent
becoming first a distant cinema screen
then a far-off house with a single lit pane.

Daniel Hardisty

MIDPOINT

The frosted four-panel glass
looks more like the fall of light
on an inside wall than a window.

In the yard's cold basin
a cord of water runs endlessly
through the hands of a fixed hose.

Beneath me, underground streams
call me by my real name
and laugh at my bed and clothes,

my man-made jeans. Here,
at night's midpoint, it is best
to avoid mirrors for fear of waking

yourself twice into the world,
a sleepwalker treading air
trapped this side of the glass.

Harry Clifton

THE PHYSICAL WORLD OF SEAMUS HEANEY

'The Physical World of Seamus Heaney' is based on the lecture delivered by Harry Clifton on 7 March 2011 at St Patrick's College, Drumcondra, D 9, as part of the sixth Seamus Heaney Lecture series, entitled *Hearing Heaney*.

I first read a poem ('Blackberry-Picking') by Seamus Heaney in secondary school in the late 1960s – off the curriculum, and well before he had become a household name. I remember it, perversely enough, because it made no impression in the conventional sense. The poetic conventions I and my generation had absorbed were high ecstatic emotion from the Romantics, national sentiment from their Irish adherents, and a singing line. A classic instance would have been the relatively early 'The Song of Wandering Aengus' by William Butler Yeats, where nature, the physical world, incandesces, spontaneously combusts under emotional pressure, into the visionary:

> I went out to the hazel wood,
> Because a fire was in my head,
> And cut and peeled a hazel wand,
> And hooked a berry to a thread;
> And when white moths were on the wing,
> And moth-like stars were flickering out,
> I dropped the berry in a stream
> And caught a little silver trout.
>
> When I had laid it on the floor
> I went to blow the fire aflame,
> But something rustled on the floor,
> And someone called me by my name:
> It had become a glimmering girl
> With apple blossom in her hair
> Who called me by my name and ran
> And faded through the brightening air

Against that background, 'Blackberry-Picking' came off as a flat, banal exercise, in a low key, talking rather than singing its way to a neatly rhymed close:

> We hoarded the fresh berries in the byre.
> But when the bath was filled we found a fur,

A rat-grey fungus, glutting on our cache.
The juice was stinking too. Once off the bush
The fruit fermented, the sweet flesh would turn sour.
I always felt like crying. It wasn't fair
That all the lovely canfuls smelt of rot.
Each year I hoped they'd keep, knew they would not.

Asked as a class what that might 'mean', it took a teacher's prompt to suggest death, evanescence, the injustice of natural processes in the inno-cent apprehension of a child. I was not alone in coming away, instead, with a sense of smudged crushed fruit in a jar, a trickle of juice, and little else. I had had, unwittingly, my first Heaney epiphany of the purely physical, ill-equipped as I then was by the curriculum to read for it or recognise it.

That, for the time being, was that. I went to university in Dublin as the Northern Irish troubles escalated, and divested myself, gradually, of the romantic nationalism I had grown up with through school and family. I would not, even then, have associated Seamus Heaney with romantic nationalism. He was clearly not a romantic, as 'Blackberry-Picking' had shown, but a mix of rural Catholic nationalism and liberal guilt, acting or writing out a conflict talked to death by elderly republicans around my post-Independence table at home. I wanted, at all costs, to find my way out of that old, embittered debate.

Not that I was uninterested in the physical, but as a child of the city I was finding it not in the Heaney of *Death of a Naturalist* or *Door into the Dark*, but in the Thomas Kinsella of *Downstream, Nightwalker and Other Poems,* and most especially *New Poems* 1973 with their evocations of Inchicore rail-sidings, Liffey quaysides, the dung and porter world of the Dublin streets, ever more exactly and Joyceanly rendered, in reaction to the romantic and the national, and with an eye, a cultural internationalism behind it, as cold and exact as Elizabeth Bishop.

For it was the metaphysical behind the physical which, at the time, excited me most – European philosophy, and in America the intellectual poetry of Wallace Stevens, underwritten by the Catholic philosophy and aesthetics of Santayana, who would die in Rome. The poet-philosopher in his Hartford attic, teasing out ideas of the world, supreme fictions. And if, after that, I needed the physical, there was the New York waterfront poetry of Hart Crane, which I could relate to my daily walks on the grain-strewn cobbles of the North Wall docks, the physical essence of central Dublin, now gone forever. The dominant myth for me then, and for many of my contemporaries, albeit with its own physical underpinning – was urban and international rather than rural and national.

It cannot be entirely forgotten, even from a distance of nearly forty years now, that another element had entered Irish poetics, mired though it was at the time in its own conflicts and historical self-preoccupations. I mean the wave of translated poetry out of Eastern Europe, the dissident aura, poetry as principled stand, with ethics, the thinking self, built into its lyrical structure. The Russians Akhmatova, Alexander Blok, Boris Pasternak, Osip Mandelstam. The revelatory selection of post-war Polish poetry, translated and introduced by a then fairly obscure Slavic Studies professor in California, Czesław Miłosz. Not only a poet himself but a thinker in poetry and about poetry. Not only a child naturalist, like Seamus Heaney, but an adult sceptical philosopher of his own death as a naturalist.

What else? The nebulous elegies of Rainer Maria Rilke, positioned, seemingly, at the end of the physical world, mourning and celebrating its disappearance inward, giving names to things as the poet's primary aim, laying claim to a vanishing earth. And in Italy the jagged irregular idiom of Eugenio Montale, a moral conscience against his own volition, wishing never to be a leader, as the beginning of the end for a lyric poet. Each and every poet with his or her own mission statement, leading away, as it seemed to me then (but not later) from the ingrown poetics of the Irish experience to a wider force-field. And all this time, Northern Ireland and its crisis in the background, unignorably there, even as my own imaginative development, inexorable and necessary, pointed me elsewhere. I remember a reading of the poem 'Funeral Rites' by Seamus Heaney, then resident in Wicklow, from his new collection *North* in a University College Dublin lecture hall in 1975 –

> Men said that he was chanting
> verses about honour
> and that four lights burned
>
> in corners of the chamber;
> which opened then, as he turned
> with a joyful face
> to look at the moon.

– and feeling no resonance, and the poet's generous inclusion of my own first poems in a little anthology – *Soundings* – of work he had chosen from younger poets. And one summer later, as he moved in from Wicklow to Dublin and I began my adult life outside Ireland altogether, a brief meeting in the dark back-room of a public house in Blackrock, and an atmosphere, on both sides, of wary approbation.

For much of the following thirty years, my own life was lived outside Ireland. And not just out of Ireland, but thousands of miles away, in Africa, Asia, later on in Europe – frames of reference where the politics, the relation to soil and weather, not to say the poetic culture, whether oral or written, were utterly different. Nonetheless, I managed to be present at the launch of *Field Work* in Trinity College in 1979, and the inaugural reading from 'Station Island' at the old Academy cinema on Pearse Street, on a cold and rainy November night in 1984. But I myself was on a different journey in those years, and the 'Heaney phenomenon' was, so to speak, happening somewhere else.

If I seem to have been talking about my own 'roots and reading', to use a Heaney expression, it is only to suggest the personal context through which his work refracted itself when eventually I came back to live in Ireland in 2004. As with the country itself, I was able to see and read the work with an unconditioned eye for not having been a part of its moral or political contexts, for actively wanting to read it now, apart from its mapping of locales, its etymologisings and stances – as a middle-aged man, married back into Irish rural life but whose physical sense of the world, as with Thomas Kinsella, had been in cities, would wish to read it, for an unmediated and redemptive feeding, as Patrick Kavanagh put it (in 'Canal Bank Walk'), of 'the gaping need of my senses':

> O unworn world enrapture me, encapture me in a web
> Of fabulous grass and eternal voices by a beech,
> Feed the gaping need of my senses, give me ad lib
> To pray unselfconsciously with overflowing speech
> For this soul needs to be honoured with a new dress woven
> From green and blue things and arguments that cannot be proven.

And yet there is all the difference in the world between a poem like that *about* the senses, and a poem, like most of Seamus Heaney's, *of* or *from* the senses. Nonetheless it is as good a point of entry as any into the physical world of Heaney if I suggest a separation between Kavanagh, essentially a moralist out of a Catholic rural tradition, European as much as Irish, going back hundreds of years, and Heaney, essentially, whether he wishes it or not, an amoralist, a poet of physical sensation on an interface between the human and the non-human, and a poet, moreover, for whom words themselves are physical sensoria.

> Sensings, mountings from the hiding places,
> Words entering almost the sense of touch,
> Ferreting themselves out of their dark hutch.
>
> [...]
>
> Vowels ploughed into other, opened ground,
> Each verse returning like the plough turned round.
>   – 'GLANMORE SONNETS'

I mentioned, not accidentally, the work of Wallace Stevens among earlier enthusiasms – that rather remote and some would say overly intellectual American poet, who lived much of his life in the dry world of insurance law, retiring upstairs after an evening meal, a drink or two and a little classical music, to the attic where he became, for a while, a separator of Heaven, Hell and Earth. Everything, not least some remarks by Heaney himself, would suggest a separation from the physical world of the Irish poet. And yet, in poetry as in everything else, there are those who lay down templates, in this case the blueprint for a possible, not yet written poetry of earth – and there are those, often decades or even generations later, who act, sometimes unconsciously, on the original suggestion, fill out the spaces, make the projected poems.

Where, in Stevens, do we find the necessary hint? I think it is in his elimination, or attempted elimination, of the elements of earthly experience that have nothing to do with earth itself, with the bare beauty of the religionless, neither infernal nor paradisal, simply there in and through the five senses:

> If only he would not pity us so much,
> Weaken our fate, relieve us of woe both great
> And small, a constant fellow of destiny,
>
> A too, too human god, self-pity's kin
> And uncourageous genesis … It seems
> As if the health of the world might be enough.
>
> It seems as if the honey of common summer
> Might be enough, as if the golden combs
> Were part of a sustenance itself enough,
>
> As if hell, so modified, had disappeared,
> As if pain, no longer satanic mimicry,
> Could be borne, as if we were sure to find our way.
> – 'ESTHÉTIQUE DU MAL'

The man who could write 'the great poems of heaven and hell have been written and the great poem of the Earth remains to be written'; or 'The greatest poverty is not to live / In a physical world' is, like Patrick Kavanagh, a moralist of the physical, not himself a physical poet. But when we read in the final poem of his *Collected Poems,* a piece entitled 'Not Ideas About The Thing But The Thing Itself', that the rising of the sun is like 'A new knowledge of reality' we are approaching the physical world of Seamus Heaney, as filtered through another influence and precursor (and friend of Stevens) the New Jersey obstetrician William Carlos Williams, whose dictum 'No ideas but in things' and whose anti-iambic, chatty quatrains, programmatically opposed to that singing line of Yeats we began with, and to the abstract religiosity of Eliot, bring us closer to the home we know in Seamus Heaney – not the home we call Ireland, but the home that is the physical world itself, bare of heaven or hell, content to dwell in its own self-sufficing household.

> There was a sunlit absence.
> The helmeted pump in the yard
> heated its iron,
> water honeyed
>
> in the slung bucket
> and the sun stood
> like a griddle cooling
> against the wall
>
> of each long afternoon.
>
> [...]
>
> here is a space
> again, the scone rising
> to the tick of two clocks.
>
> And here is love
> like a tinsmith's scoop
> sunk past its gleam
> in the meal-bin.
> – 'SUNLIGHT'

The 'sunlit absence' and the 'love...sunk past its gleam' in that poem are, in at least one sense, a world stripped of any aura other than the purely physical, with the shine of transcendence taken off it, bathed only in its own sunlit immanence. A homely yet tremendous immanence, like the bare winter garden in Stevens's 'The Plain Sense of Things' where 'a fantastic effort has failed' and there are only dead leaves, a rat entering a pond, a few denuded trees to be seen, and which is in a strange way celebrated by the naked, newly emancipated eye. But celebrated not in the fluent iambics of Stevens, but the short colloquial lines of Williams, with the single word, like a physical act, given its maximum plosive and explosive force.

Heaney himself has spoken of his indebtedness to the hard factuality and spokenness of Williams, and I myself have invoked Stevens. But the

Irish poet's sojourn in California in the academic year 1970-71 clearly exposed him to other influences where a human interface with nature and the physical is concerned, notably the poems of Gary Snyder, which read like a field notation of the senses, when the 'myths and texts' that mediate between the man and the American wilderness have been stripped away, and all that is left is the bare cosmic space of the physical universe itself, and the man alone in it, thirsting, as in the wilderness poem 'Milton by Firelight', for some taproot back into human culture:

> 'Oh hell, what do mine eyes
> with grief behold?'

> [...]

> What use, Milton, a silly story
> Of our lost general parents,
> eaters of fruit?

> [...]

> In ten thousand years the Sierras
> Will be dry and dead, home of the scorpion.
> Ice-scratched slabs and bent trees.
> No paradise, no fall,
> Only the weathering land
> The wheeling sky,
> Man and his Satan
> Scouring the chaos of the mind.
> Oh hell!

A world not so much hostile as indifferent to man, whether as individual or species, and the more frightening for that, a landscape out of which the wilderness poet Robinson Jeffers, perched on the edge of the Pacific in his tower at Carmel, could write of that ocean as 'a vast eye' staring out into the cosmos, seeing nothing of human affairs, and where Heaney, himself resident in California, could write of 'the empty amphitheatre of the west.'

If I mention Jeffers, it is not simply for the 'inhumanism' as it has been called, of his turning away from society and politics to live by the Pacific, but for his connection with another poet resident by that ocean, the already mentioned Polish expatriate Czesław Miłosz, so central later on to Seamus Heaney, though seemingly they had yet to meet. Miłosz of course is a whole story in himself, but I want, in this context, to focus on just two aspects. The first, and it goes back to Kavanagh's 'gaping need of the senses', is the gradual disappearance of the physical, the atrophy of touch, taste, smell, the blurring of eye and ear, as the modern world turns abstract, not to say virtual.

> Roads on concrete pillars, cities of glass and cast iron,
> Airfields larger than tribal dominions
> Suddenly ran short of their essence and disintegrated.
> Not in a dream but really, for, subtracted from themselves,
> They could only hold on as do things which should not last.
> Out of trees, field stones, even lemons on the table,
> Materiality escaped and their spectrum
> Proved to be a void, a haze on a film.
> Dispossessed of its objects, space was swarming.
> Everywhere was nowhere, and nowhere everywhere.
>   – 'OECONOMIA DIVINA'

That might be taken for the dismay of an Old World poet in the New World, were it not that the same had already been said in the Old World, by Rilke, who had written 'Everything is disappearing inwards'. And it is the counter-impulse to that which brings readers to the physical world of Seamus Heaney – past the myth-making and the politics, to something more essential, not only to themselves but to the poet also. A fallback zone, an irreducible realm of the senses, that comes to the rescue again and again, and tells him, like the inner voice in his poem 'North', where his real self lies:

> It said, 'Lie down
> in the word-hoard, burrow
> the coil and gleam
> of your furrowed brain.
>
> Compose in darkness.
> Expect aurora borealis
> in the long foray
> but no cascade of light.
>
> Keep your eye clear
> as the bleb of an icicle,
> trust the feel of what nubbed treasure
> your hands have known.'

The other aspect of Miłosz, for my purpose here, is that he shares with Heaney the 'death of a naturalist' experience of the boy forced to grow beyond the jamjar-on-a-windowsill romanticisings of a collector of beauties, to the truth about nature as a morally neutral killing-ground of slime kings whose blunt heads fart, of kittens unwanted in sacks at the bottom of rivers, and the zip-cold otherness of oceans entered into for swimming lessons. That sense of recoil at the amoral is explicit, too, in Miłosz's abhorrence of nature documentaries, their beautifying and humanising of a mesh of violence and death. In Heaney, that identification with, and horror at, the physical world, demands a more complex reading, and for that we have to go back briefly to the Seventies.

I mentioned earlier, as part of my student reading, the Modern European poets in Translation series. Miłosz of course, as well as Mandelstam, Herbert and others. No one should underestimate the effect of these sometimes rough, even banal translations on the then poetic scene in Ireland, less for reasons of language than for their examples of moral leadership, hardly a quality demanded of poets in the bohemian public house world of Dublin and London in the Fifties and Sixties, and roundly repudiated by Patrick Kavanagh in his poem 'The Hero':

> He was an ordinary man, a man full of humour,
> Born for no high sacrifice, to be no marble god;
> But all the gods had failed that harvest and someone spread the rumour
> That he might be deluded into taking on the job.
> And they came to him in the Spring
> And said: you are our poet-king.
>
> Their evil weakness smiled on him and he had no answer to it,
> They drove him out of corners into the public gaze;
> And the more he tried to defend himself the more they cried, O poet
> Why must you always insult us when we only want to praise?
> And he said: I wish you would
> Pick on someone else to be your god.

In the traumatised Ireland of the Seventies, however, the situation seemed to demand a responsible and careful poetic figurehead, rather than anti-heroic opters-out on the periphery, cultivating their otherness. A figure not just Irish but a product of the Age of Moderation that had replaced, in poetry as in other areas of the mind, the Age of Extremes, the release of energy in all directions, often with devastating effect, in the earlier part of the twentieth century. That figure, initially in Ireland, latterly and more generally in the intellectual West, was Seamus Heaney. This is not the place, nor is it my intention in this context, to explore the ups and downs of a public destiny, merely to state that it was vested in that one person at that time, and has been carried through, not without consequences for what I take to be his primary world.

Here are two examples, from that earth-world overlaid with moral abstraction. In a poem for the Dutch potter Sonja Landweer we get, in its first section, an evocation of a deliquescent otherworld in and for itself:

> The soils I knew ran dirty. River sand
> Was the one clean thing that stayed itself
> In that slabbery, clabbery, wintry, puddled ground.
>
> Until I found Bann clay. Like wet daylight
> Or viscous satin under the felt and frieze
> Of humus layers. The true diatomite
>
> Discovered in a little sucky hole,
> Grey-blue, dull-shining, scentless, touchable –
> Like the earth's old ointment box, sticky and cool.

In subsequent sections, however, the voice, or voice-over, becomes an exalted but formulaic expression of historical optimism, the rhetoric of schoolday speeches, commencement addresses:

> To have lived it through and now be free to give
> Utterance, body and soul – to wake and know
> Every time that it's gone for good, the thing
> That nearly broke you –
>
> Is worth it all, the five years on the rack,
> The fighting back, the being resigned, and not
> One of the unborn will appreciate
> Freedom like this ever

Again, in a poem called 'Weighing In' invoking the cold force of gravity itself, we get an evocation of something purely extraneous to the human, let alone the socially or politically moral:

> The 56 lb. weight. A solid iron
> Unit of negation. Stamped and cast
> With an inset, rung-thick, moulded, short crossbar
>
> For a handle. Squared-off and harmless-looking
> Until you tried to lift it, then a socket-ripping,
> Life-belittling force...

Followed, in subsequent sections, by the voice-over of the socially moral, taking the cold primary material, in this case weight, gravity itself, and making of it something like a sermon:

> And this is all the good tidings amount to:
> This principle of bearing, bearing up
> And bearing out, just having to
>
> Balance the intolerable in others
> Against our own, having to abide
> Whatever we settled for and settled into
>
> Against our better judgement. Passive
> Suffering makes the world go round.
> Peace on earth, men of good will, all that
>
> Holds good only as long as the balance holds…

The first voice in both these poems, and I could quote many others, seems to me the authentic voice of the poet, writing out of his primary world. The second is a kind of voice-over, hortatory, programmatically positive, urging the human race along the straight and narrow of willed wholesomeness. Never completely convincing in itself – Heaney is too much the poet of sensation to yield to the tone of moral certitude we get in Patrick Kavanagh – it feels imposed on the poet like the leadership role itself, accepted but with scepticism, getting in the way of something more essential, more truly redemptive:

> And there I was, incredible to myself
> among people far too eager to believe me
> and my story, even if it happened to be true.
>   – 'SWEENEY REDIVIVUS'

Invoking the redemptive, though, means leaving behind that uneasy interface between nature and morality and entering the realm of the sacred, where Seamus Heaney shades over into Ted Hughes, a poet with whom he shares a genius for the physical, but with, I think, crucial divergences. Here, and it is merely one example, are lines about water from Hughes' poem 'The River':

> So the river is a god
>
> Knee-deep among reeds, watching men,
> Or hung by the heels down the door of a dam

It is a god, and inviolable.
Immortal. And will wash itself of all deaths.

And here are lines about water from Seamus Heaney's poem 'Undine':

...I swallowed his trench

Gratefully, dispersing myself for love
Down in his roots, climbing his brassy grain –
But once he knew my welcome, I alone

Could give him subtle increase and reflection.
He explored me so completely, each limb
Lost its cold freedom. Human, warmed to him.

In 'The River' we are in a sacred non-human realm in which man is an unclean intrusion. In 'Undine' there is a humanising of the physical, a co-opting of water into the life and work of man. It is as if these two poets, so close in one way, are facing in opposite directions. Or are they, as I prefer to think, one poet with two faces, into the non-human sacred in one case, into the human and the social in the other? The respective fates of these two genii of the physical, or these two aspects of one and the same poet, would appear to bear this out. Hughes, anathematised as a witch, a dealer in dark forces for their own sake. Heaney, in his own words 'doomed to the decent thing' as a leader of men, a bringer-over of the physical into the diminished, even sanitised realm of social morality.

I hope by now my account of my own roots and reading, the mental world of a student in the Seventies, will not have seemed irrelevant. Stevens, Rilke, Miłosz – all, like myself, extraneous to the national, or in the good sense, parochial, aspects of Seamus Heaney, and for that very reason with an angle of vision on what is most universal in his work, the evocation of the physical.

The American poet Allen Ginsberg once said that to descend into your own body was harder than to go to the moon. I have not travelled that far, but I have travelled, been, as I said, on my own journey through ethics and politics, body and spirit, and having come back, in middle age, with its 'gaping need of the senses' I know again what I have already known elsewhere, that all homecomings are to the physical, and that this, beyond all the necessary self-positionings, is what in the work of Seamus Heaney will last. Not the politics, not the moral stances, but that half-forgotten, unforgettable smudge of fruit in a jamjar.

Jaki McCarrick

CAMOMILE

Fair fur-headed sisters
all on one woody stem,

my mother would gather
your blonde-dye heads

from the parks of Kilburn
and Hampstead, and boil you up:

gold for her hair
and for her children's

though I was dark
as a secret.

Your bombshells
sweeten the air.

As infusion of your whole
dried body calms

the unquiet part of the heart
and worries kidney stones.

From the Greek *khamaimelon*,
meaning 'earth-apple',

your yellow melon-heads
indiscriminately perfume

battlefields
as they do suburban lawns –

and bring today
to this cluttered desk

my mother,
that platinum-haired apothecary.

Lynne Edgar

MUSING

She thought
curiosity a curious thing.
Especially that it could kill...
A bit like excess, she supposed.
Sidelining premier contenders –
cigarettes, vodka...under certain circumstances,
sex, according to *The Daily Record* –
she thought of baggage,
excess of which was a nuisance for Ruby
returning from Bruges' Christmas market.
But a bigger inconvenience:
Five killed on escalator –
Tragedy as over-laden traveller topples.
'Five dominoed dead
in a spat with a fat suitcase',
she said to herself...
'It's feasible'.

Jane Yeh

THE LILIES

The lilies whisper but no-one is listening.
Their heads are filled with pollen and boredom.
In the gaps between them, anything could happen
(But it doesn't). Their mouths are filled with sugar and organs.

In the parlour they crowd out the normal flowers
With their fussy ways and *pudeur*. It's a hollow victory.
They lean against the wall like spinsters on crutches.
They think about wishbones and what happened yesterday (nothing).

The lilies are throwing a party for themselves.
Their eyes light up at the thought of company.
There will be a finger buffet, with cocktail sticks for the squeamish.
Their stems will be filled with pity and vodka.

Later there will be parts falling off. The freakish lilies
Sulk and droop in their vases like limp spaghetti.
They don't expect much, but they're still disappointed.
The water they drink tastes sour like it.

Jane Yeh

THE MERLINS

You've no neck at all, just mouth then gullet.
Necklessness makes the silhouette so elegant.

Your neat head set with a diamond beak
Is a one-piece machine. Too bad you can't kiss with it.

In the universe, everything is prey
To your will. How rapturous it must feel

To preen on an icy Scandinavian branch. Have
A care – your claws could fillet a rat in its sleep. The poor

Relations you exceed just feed on your scraps. It's a far
Cry from the regurgitated worms of your youth.

Merlins, when your coop is flown the searchers won't
Be able to pluck out the unspoiled yolks

Of your hearts, or pinch your young. Where
The rats and goblins live, in the lower regions, there –

You'll squawk and perch and make a jolly home.
You'll rule the roost. You'll sweep them all clean.

You're like the cat who got the cream and then
Took everyone else's cream. We think you're boring.

Jane Yeh

LACE

> *Which one of you bitches is my mother?*
>> – from the miniseries *Lace*, teleplay by Elliott Baker

Everyone thinks my French accent's a fake.
Bitches, you left me in Bourgogne to rot
Like a sour grape – cut off from the vine.
You danced, drank champagne, grew famous, forgot

I was being raised by peasants on crusts
And dirt. I clawed my way out of that hellhole
Through guile and sex. I made a fortune
In films lying flat on my back. I stole

Your sons' hearts, then crushed them, just because I'm bad.
Bitches, you made me what I am today:
A gold-digging tramp in Lycra and furs

Who's waited a lifetime to make you pay.
But a catfight? That's so Eighties. No more
Drama, *maman* – I just want to be loved.

Sarah Collins

THE OWL PELLET

Everything held here:
mouse bones, paper thin,
a bead of corn lit yellow
in dark peat, one feather,
a stray bog cotton thread, silken
with evening light, as
two streaks of grass tease apart
the owl's arc of day and night,
how she paints curves of land, a wash
of speckled sand, the grainy earth
in a vole's pelt stippled with heather
and peat slush, oats thrown wide
from the combine –

almost too much to take in.

Miriam Gamble

PRÉCIS

Cast on the beach,
        a momentary attraction;

erstwhile Goliath of the sea
        now the property

of the Lord Paramount of Constable,
        the rotting body his to sell;

which swell
        designates its fate not

the cooking pot but
        a series of pits,

the proud flesh there
        to await reaction,

the skull emptied of its fluid;
        It lights, beneficent,

towns with its bulbous head –
        lights the taverns, the assizes,

the conversations of the great and good
        while its massive carcass moulds;

is raised
        when skeletons

are *á la mode*,
        becomes a temporary hit

then a lone child's playground
        apparatus, animal shit

Miriam Gamble

AN EMBLEM THEREOF

Like Neanderthal man in his cairn
I have found myself here, face to the wall,
curled underneath the bounty of a duvet
which, though reeking of sex,
has been dubbed both a burial shroud and a caul.

How they weep, and tear at their hair!
How I hold fire, obstinately foetal.
They try the gods, but their prayers sway
weakly on the wind – they know this is no hex –
retreat into their mouths again, irresolute and fatal.

And sure enough, the word comes down
and in doing so confirms their worst suspicions:
Sorry folks; the next move is her own...

A civil war starts over who invented manumission.
It lasts x years, during which time I stay
in the duvet, scan Proust, cultivate the wax in my ears.

Miriam Gamble

DRESSING FLEAS

If we do not mass produce products, we vie with one another
in the difficult, exquisite and useless art of dressing fleas
        – Octavio Paz

Mr and Mrs Flea are dressed up
and ready for the celebrations.
He sports a neatly tailored waistcoat,
she silver-bordered asymmetric skirts.

They are the talk and toast of the party.

Sad to say, however,
a budding fashionista in the audience
catches sight of their duds,
and next year on the catwalks of Milan and London
the look is brazenly passed off
as the signature of the couture line
at the brand new *House of Insect*,
which in due course signs a cracking deal
with a high street shop.

I don't need to say the Fleas never see a penny,
and neither does their tailor,
who, five months out of the punishing year,
wrecks his eyes
and racks sleep-heavy brains
in the decking out of his favourite customers.

Though for him it was never about the money –
the fleas, dearest, could hardly pay,
and the tailor is in any case not a tailor
but a farmer from the provinces
going about satisfaction in his own, yes,
                            his own unfathomable way
where the sun drops, faithless, to the littoral,
dead dark balling its fists against the light.

See him there, readied at the chipboard table.
He takes a swig of liquor.
See, dearest, how the inconsistent starts glitter and claw.

Caitríona Ní Chléirchín

DOIRE NA SEALG

Rachaidh mé síos go Doire na Sealg,
áit a mbeidh mo ghrá
faoi chiamhair chraobh.

Beidh dearcáin faoi chos is caonach
i lár na coille cumhra,
caora cuilinn, cnó agus úlla
go fairsing ann.
Biolar agus samhadh
i ngleann ceo.
Flúirse ina bhflúirse ann.
Fianna a ritheann i réimeanna is
damh sa choill,
amuigh ar an cheo sa choill.
Buailfidh muid lenár dtaibhsí féin.

Luífidh muid faoin chrann caorthainn ann
ag éisteacht le monabhar an tsrutháin
is craobhmhúr agus craobhcheathanna
craobhchith tamall ón spéir.

Binn guth an smólaigh ar bharra craobh ann
binn guth na cuaiche
is an loin dhuibh.

Glaise ina ghlaise ann.
Duileabhar fúinn is luachra
go barra glún.

Éalóidh muid ón domhan seal.
Éalóidh muid uainn féin
i lár na coille cumhra,
caora cuilinn cnó agus úlla
go fairsing ann
biolar agus samhadh
i ngleann ceo.

Seinnfidh ceol do shúl im chroí, a stór
nuair a rachaidh muid síos go Doire na Sealg
le coimheascar lae.

Tá caonach faoi chos i nDoire na Sealg
mar a luíonn muid faoi chiamhar chraobh
i nDoire na Sealg, ba bhrídeach sí mé
is lean mé mo ghrá mar eilit sa cheo.

Caitríona Ní Chléirchín

DERNASHALLOG

I will go down to Dernashallog,
the wood of the hunting,
down to where my love will be
under the gloom of branches

There'll be acorns underfoot and moss
in the middle of the fragrant wood
holly berries, nuts and apples
in plenty there
cress and sorrel
in the mist-glen
plentifulness there
and deers running in leaps
and a stag out in the wood mist
We'll meet our own ghosts there

We'll lie a while under the rowan tree
listening to the stream's murmur
rain showers through the branches
awhile from the sky

The thrushes voice will be sweet there,
from the top of every branch
and sweet the cuckoo
sweet the blackbird

Greeness there beneath us,
leaves and rushes
up to our knees

We'll escape from the world awhile
escape from ourselves
in the middle of the fragrant wood
holly berries, nuts and apples
in plenty there
cress and sorrel
in the mist-glen

The music of your eye
will play in my heart, love
when we go down to Dernashallog
the wood of the hunting
at dusky eveningtide

There's moss underfoot in Dernashallog
where we lie under the shade of branches
In Dernashallog, I was a fairy bride
and I followed my love like a doe in the mist

– translation of 'Doire na Sealg'

Caitríona Ní Chléirchín

SCARADH NA GCOMPÁNACH
 – as sraith de dhánta ar Imeacht na n-Iarlaí

Labhrann Caitríona Nic Aonghusa, Cuntaois Thír Eoghain:

Ar bhruach an Fheabhail, tuar
tagann chugam, i ndtaibreamh:
glaoim oraibh, a fheara, d' impí –
an imeacht seo, ní tairbheach.

Mar a scaipfear an deatach,
is amhlaidh a scaipfear:
mar chéir i láthair na tine,
is amhlaidh a leáfar.

Insint ag caoineadh gaoithe
ar a bhfuil i ndán dúinn
sa leabhar ag an fhiach dubh
nó pianphás i dTúr Londan.

Mo mhac óg, mo mhuirnín Conn
mo leanbh féin, mo laochsa
gan é ach a cúig de bhlianta faram
is gach aon snáth le réabadh

Fonn a bhí orm, ón chéad lá riamh
éirí den turas go Rath Maoláin
ach bhagair m'Iarla orm gabháil ar aghaidh
agus ár mac a fhágáil i lámha an strainséara.

Caitríona Ní Chléirchín

THE PARTING OF THE COMRADES
  – from a series of poems on The Flight of the Earls

Caitríona Magennis, Countess of Tyrone, speaks:

On the bank of the Foyle,
A sign in a dream I saw:
I call to you, men, beseeching–
Without benefit, this leaving.

As smoke is dispersed
We'll be dispersed ourselves
Like wax in the flame
We will melt away.

The wind's wailing relates
What will be our fate,
In the book of the black raven
Or agony in the Tower of London.

My darling Conn, my young son,
My hero and my only one,
Only with me five years all told,
And every thread is to be torn.

From the very first it was my urge
To quit this journey to Rathmullen:
But my Earl had me carry on
And with a stranger leave our son.

  – translation of 'Scaradh na gCompánach' by **Colm Breathnach**

James Owens

HARD RAIN BEHIND A SCREEN OF THISTLES

It was not this mean spring cold seeping under the doors
but a summer cloudburst when we stopped the car,
obeying the ache that twisted through our nerves that year,
and touched naked on the thick grass, secret
behind a row of thistle and clotted blackberry.
Rainwater was the taste of July sky licked from your thighs,
sopping our hair, streaming off your breasts, off my shoulders.
If I remembered a story about rain, would that be a way back?

Later, in the afternoon, after watching more rain fall,
I think I should have said it was like a baptism.
Seeing us there, discovering those two hidden in the long grass,
would it seem that our whole bodies were weeping
the fat warm rain, movements tensing fast to a shared cry
lost in thunder, our bellies together, as slick as newborns?

Rabindranath Tagore

The following selection of Tagore's aphorisms is taken from
Stray Birds / Éanlaith Strae, an edition with Irish versions by **Gabriel
Rosenstock**, forthcoming from Salmon Poetry to celebrate the
150th anniversary of the birth of Tagore. The English versions are
Tagore's own.

ÉANLAITH strae an tsamhraidh chun na fuinneoige chugam:
eitlíonn leo.
Duilliúr buí an fhómhair, ní chanann, ar foluain, ag titim: osna.

STRAY birds of summer come to my window to sing and fly away.
And yellow leaves of autumn, which have no songs, flutter and fall
there with a sigh.

~

COMPÁNTAS fhánaithe beaga an tsaoil, fágaíg' rian bhur gcos ar
mo bhriathra.

O TROUPE of little vagrants of the world, leave your footprints in
my words.

~

CÉN teanga a labhrann tú, a mhuir?
Teanga na ceiste síoraí.
Cén teanga ina bhfuil do fhreagra, a spéir?
Teanga an tosta gan chríoch.

'WHAT language is thine, O sea?'
  'The language of eternal question.'
'What language is thy answer, O sky?'
  'The language of eternal silence.'

~

SUÍM san fhuinneog an mhaidin seo is gabhann an saol thar bráid,
stopann seal,
sméideann a cheann orm, imíonn.

I SIT at my window this morning where the world like a passer-by
stops for a moment, nods to me and goes.

~

Ní fheiceann tú an rud is ea thú; is é do scáth an ní a fheiceann tú.

WHAT you are you do not see, what you see is your shadow.

~

TAGANN na crainn go dtí an fhuinneog chugam, guth tnúthánach an domhain bhailbh.

THE trees come up to my window like the yearning voice of the dumb earth.

~

IS ionadh le Dia gach maidin nua aige.

HIS own mornings are new surprises to God.

~

BA mhaith leis an éan a bheith ina néal. Ba mhaith leis an néal a bheith ina éan.

THE bird wishes it were a cloud. The cloud wishes it were a bird.

~

CANANN an t-eas, 'Ailleog cheoil a aimsím nuair a aimsím mo shaoirse.'

THE waterfall sings, 'I find my song, when I find my freedom.'

~

NÍLIM in ann a rá cad a chuir an croí tostmhar seo ag meath le cumha i ndiaidh na riachtanas beag sin nach n-iarrann sé, nach eol dó, nach cuimhin leis.

I CANNOT tell why this heart languishes in silence.
It is for small needs it never asks, or knows or remembers.

~

DÁLA mhianta an domhain, bíonn na crainn ar a mbarraicíní chun spléachadh a fháil ar Neamh.

THE trees, like the longings of the earth, stand a-tiptoe to peep at the heaven.

~

IS déithe aige iad a chuid uirlisí troda. Nuair a bhuann a chuid uirlisí troda cloítear eisean.

HE has made his weapons his gods. When his weapons win he is defeated himself.

~

AGUS caille uirthi, leanann an Scáil an Solas go ceansa rúnda, le coiscéimeanna ciúine an ghrá.

SHADOW, with her veil drawn, follows Light in secret meekness, with her silent steps of love.

~

NÍL eagla ar réaltaí a bheith ina lampróga.

THE stars are not afraid to appear like fireflies.

~

TÁ mo lá-sa caite, bád a tarraingíodh isteach ar an trá mé, ag éisteacht le ceol rince na taoide um thráthnóna.

MY day is done, and I am like a boat drawn on the beach, listening to the dance-music of the tide in the evening.

~

NÁ scanraíodh móimintí thú – is mar sin a chanann glór na síoraíochta.

NEVER be afraid of the moments – thus sings the voice of the everlasting.

~

IS le grá don ní atá Neamhfhoirfe a ghléasann an ní atá Foirfe go niamhrach.

THE Perfect decks itself in beauty for the love of the Imperfect.

~

ÉIRÍONN Dia cortha de ríochtaí ach ní éiríonn riamh cortha de bhláthanna beaga.

GOD grows weary of great kingdoms, but never of little flowers.

Matthew Geden

DOUBTING THOMAS

Beatific that smile crossing the possible,
raised from the dark dead earth,
steady in the sunlight a hand
reaches out. Touch, a gaping blemish
in the smooth skin. It can never
be said, what went on between
the two of us, those moments
have long passed understanding.
We might have gone to Moscow
in the Cold War, wandered
the snow-struck streets, gazed
into the eyes of our lost leader.

Matthew Geden

TOM COURTENAY, PHILIP LARKIN AND THE BUTTERFLY

'Am I a man who dreamt of being a butterfly, or am I a butterfly dreaming
that I am a man?
            – Chuang Tzu

He is in the midst of death,
or life as some of us prefer,
when out of the air and under the light
a butterfly rises and falls onto the page
like a pause painted in the margins.
We watch as it spreads its orange wings,
a flutter of light in the darkness,
a message delivered to the gods.

Kate Noakes

THE WORK-BENCH VICE MORALITY TEST

For this final part of the medical, it helps
if you can relax as much as possible.
Try just being still –

He clamps my head in a phrenology device,
gauges a gnomon to angle
the lamp, takes a magnifying glass

and in the raking light, begins his search
for tension and hidden things. Each time
he pauses to make a small sound

or slight expression, I know he's seen it,
oblique and warped, there in the slant
texture of my face, in valleys and shadows,

wrinkles, cracks; all the signs and stigmata
of my drudge skin, imprinted there
for the reading and he's learned

the language well. Nothing's secret,
nothing held in. I'm at his whim as he notes
these changes of mind and direction. How

will he report my sanity? Will he reveal
my imperfect soul 'til now so well
concealed? I'm his pet experiment,

his magic lantern show. He has to unmask
my story, my fake designs, the palimpsest
I've made. I need him to put these

distortions down to craquelure and age,
nothing sinister, nothing like a true
reflection. I need this job.

Vona Groarke

IS IT TIME?

The children will be waiting for me
with blue veined arms and all tomorrow
slaked in the whites of their eyes.

They have knowledge, they assure me,
of how rain comes undone
and mornings thicken like milk.

And they remember the story of the night
that popped itself inside out
and forgot all of its songs.

'But what happened the moon?'
Picked up, shiny penny, by a woman
with too much air in her pockets,

spent on a word from a barrow-seller
and gifted, in turn, to a boy and a girl
who learn what becomes of it.

Vona Groarke

FURROW

Though scooped with my printed fingers
and lined with remnants of ink

the furrow's trench-like depression
knows nothing, or almost nothing,

of the barrow's burial mound. Pages flutter
between them, ornamentally

and it is only a matter of sound
before elision, or collapse.

Into which, complicitly,
I would ease myself

but for what I'm not allowed say;
would lay down my head in furlough nouns

that have shed every memory of you.
But there I will not lie again.

There is at stake an honesty
in knowing, definitively, what is meant

by walking into a moment
and taking the measure of it,

of what the first hand might have to declare
if the second weren't so loud,

of how they occupy each other,
to arrive at a single end.

How little I comprehend any of this,
the faithless slippage of things.

How years, like words, silt up in themselves:
how, when I'm taking the bus home,

I'm also hitchhiking to years ago
to fill in both our names on a form

or am sitting at a yellow table
in a restaurant called *Now*.

You have come on foot to visit
and I am waiting for you.

Vona Groarke

INTERVAL

Between acts, mindful
of the present tense
but beholden to what
has already occurred
or what might be going to

as a noun between two verbs
comes to depend on them both
until there is quiet enough
for the next thing to happen
and be happening again

in the way the opening note
of the second half
has the last note by heart
but doesn't either recall or predict
what plays out over time.

Better to aspire
to knowing as much
of what's done and
what remains to be done
as the pure note on the violin

knows about purfling
or applause, or about
the mastodon tusk
or Mongolian mare's tail
that goes into making the bow.

Tom French

LEAVING BALLYBEG

The slowed-down striptease of September has begun
to turn our thoughts from sun to cold again.
The sea tonight throws seaweed up in tons
and, shrinking again into the bearable cold,
I think of you tonight, of how we've grown

estranged because I became *a spiritual drain*
on your rustic idyll with its own fresh well,
where the masonry nail I buried in the gable
to hang my *Flight into Egypt* was as close
to a permanent gesture as I was able to come;

of you, wolf-whistling in the doorway at 4 a.m.
for your loved collie, touring the townlands
and turning back on her tracks to head for home;
of the shock of the sound of you in your room,
your heart-rending, existential grief that left me

capable of little else except making more tea;
of your landlord who can't bring himself to sell
on account of his ties to the place, his habit
of waving a work-thickened finger at the front
bedroom door and declaiming, *'Seventy year ago,*

my mother, behind that door, had me', dropping
the plural (but not to sound more country).
Which of us, Éamon, could say the same?
Or – for that matter – wants to? There's hardly
room to swing a cat in there, let alone have Pat.

What ever became of that gallant little Belgian
who preceded me? Of the plans he harboured
to petition for a dehumidifier? The neck!
Then vanishing within months because of damp.
He must've considered the oar that wedged

the bed in place no stranger than the bone shaker
hanging by its handlebars from the outhouse rafters
among the kitchen chairs and thatcher's ladders,
or the apple tree in summer hung with clothes
'to give them some air', brought in when it snowed;

or – come to think of it – that hitcher you picked up
and brought home, who was hell-bent on swopping
his Fatherland of Fear for our Free State of Yeats
to elude conscription into the nuclear age, whose ruck-
sack was packed with laundry and philosophy.

Remember the pilgrimage he made to Rossroe,
boldly going where no man in his right mind would go,
where Wittgenstein lived in the last pool of darkness
in Europe, converted into a fish farm since,
where the limits of language were a razor wire fence

and the security enquired if he could read English.
Tonight is *Cine Club* night and you are abroad
at the east-facing gable, twiddling a pair of rabbit's
ears in the hopes of a film on TG4 or RTÉ
by one of the great *Ks* – *Kieślowski, Kiarostami,*

(and the other two who always elude me),
at the place where your garden came up trumps
that legendary summer when the sun won tenure
for months, and you took pains to empty presses
of bedspreads and linen to range fat tomatoes

on the slats to ripen; but, living in the dip between
two hills, all that antique *Bush* could pick up was
angelus bells in a blizzard, as if some station
had taken to airing the director's cut of *Carry On
Up To Antarctica* and screened on a loop that clip

of Kenneth Williams who, walking a fine line
between altruism and misanthropy, pops out
for a split second to answer a call of nature
and stops there for eternity. You could hardly,
Éamon, say the same for me. By the time

I write again or you get this note, having flogged
more boxes of novels to lighten the load
but hung on to the slim volumes that would weigh
any old *Starlet* down to her arches, I will have
smoothed my creases from the undersheet

and wedged the window open to clear the air.
I thought it would be as easy as striking camp
but now that the time to leave is here it dawns –
Emir Kusturica, *Akira Kurosawa* – I am leaving home,
going as I came, under my own steam.

Tom Duddy

JOHN CLARE AND THE POETRY OF BIRDS

It is no surprise that one of the most recent anthologies of bird poetry, *The Poetry of Birds* (2009), edited by Simon Armitage and Tim Dee, contains more poems by John Clare than any other poet. Such, indeed, is the strength of Clare's contribution to this particular sub-genre of nature poetry that anthologists have sometimes felt obliged to treat his poems as a significant turning point in the evolution of nature poetry, representing a significant breakthrough in terms of realistic attention to detail and a determination to tell the truth precisely as the observer sees it, without recourse to conventional assumptions or stereotypes. Perhaps the most radical acknowledgement of the significance of Clare's naturalism is that expressed by Mike Mockler in the introduction to his illustrated anthology, *Flights of Imagination* (1982), in which he describes Clare as 'the first nature poet in the true sense', the first English poet 'to present nature pictorially, lovingly, accurately and knowledgeably'. Clare is a true nature poet in the measure that nature prompted him to write 'not about himself or his feelings, but about what he actually saw in the fields and woods around his Northampton home'.[1] Clare's poems represent for Mockler such a pivotal development in the history of nature poetry that he is prepared to extrapolate from them a criterion by which he will pass rather harsh judgment on the work of earlier nature poets, including even Wordsworth. Mockler in fact refuses to include anything by Wordsworth in his book. His somewhat summary reasoning is that nature for Wordsworth is an abstract, personified force, and not something that exists wildly independently of the poet, to which the poet finds himself responding observantly and joyfully. In particular, the birds that Wordsworth describes 'exist only as far as they affect the poet or those close to him'. In the case of such well-known bird poems as 'To the Cuckoo', 'The Green Linnet' and 'To a Skylark', the bird in question is no more than 'a starting point for a train of thought or an outpouring of emotion'.[2] Mockler's preference is for poems that present birds 'as they are, rather than to use them as symbols to point to some moral about life or human behaviour'.[3] It is Clare who shows the way in the realisation of this project of joyful, honest-to-nature observation, and does so in a way that exposes the deficiencies of other 'nature' poets.

A rather less radical view of Clare's position in the history of bird poetry is taken by Peggy Munsterberg in her scholarly, long-ranging and considered introduction to the *Penguin Book of Bird Poetry* (1980). In her introduction she shows the extent to which bird poetry has changed in response to changes in both the wider culture and in the history of poetry itself. More than perhaps any other non-human creature, birds have been the subject of superstition, fable, myth, legend and folklore. Indeed, part of the story of the evolution of bird poetry is its gradual extrication from the cultural tangle of conventional belief and assumption. When birds feature in pre-modern poetry, it is very much as bearers of signs, omens, or other symbolic meanings of one kind or another. Birds in Anglo-Saxon verse are treated for the most part as the means to a symbolic or allegorical end, often of a negative kind. The raven, for example, is nothing if not always ominous, sometimes cast in an auspicious light but more often taken to prefigure death or war. Medieval bird poetry, according to Munsterberg, broke with the earlier traditions of 'omenism' by creating a space for the nightingale and other singing birds. Even where new birds of prey are introduced, they are characterised in a more complex symbolic way, offering a spectrum of meanings that range from the marking of hierarchy (in nature and socie-ty) to the celebration of courtly love. The falcon sits close to the top of a 'natural' hierarchy, like the lordly eagle, but it is also allocated to a more figurative role as the (male) lover who hunts his desired prey. Perhaps Munsterberg's most unexpected observation on the medieval treatment of birds is that there is a new element of realism in the manner in which birds are represented, despite the usually anthropomorphic character of these representations. In the early thirteenth-century poem, *The Owl and the Nightingale*, for example, though not at all an attempt to treat the named birds in a descriptive manner, there is nonetheless 'a real fusion of the animal and the human'. The poem consists of a lengthy debate between the birds about the relative merits of each other's voices, especially with regard to their effects on the human world, with each bird singing its own praises while finding fault with the supposed virtues of its opponent.

The achievement of the anonymous poet is to make the human characters of the birds 'come out of the bird nature',[4] in the sense that the steadfastness advised by the owl is grounded in the fact of its all-year residence in its local habitat and also in the fact that it continues to 'sing', even in winter, unlike the more 'flighty' nightingale who opts to spend winter elsewhere. The nightingale's more carefree, light-hearted outlook on life resonates with a natural cycle that is indeed less earth-bound and given to flight in more ways than one. Even as the debating birds try to represent each other's virtues as vices, with reference to physique, 'voice', and manners, they inadvertently succeed in giving moderately realistic characterisations of each other. Of course, the realism here is much qualified by the fact that these talking birds are ultimately no more than fanciful enlargements of human beings. Even in Chaucer's verse, birds are effectively human characters in bird-like guises.

In Elizabethan poetry, according to Munsterberg, we find ourselves at an increasing distance from the ominous birds of Old English verse. Here the birds that feature most prominently are the singers or choristers, whose presence in poetry reflects certain developments in the wider culture. Munsterberg suggests that the liveliest bird-song poems were written between the 1580s and the 1620s, 'a period which corresponds to the flowering of the English Madrigal School'. Yet, despite the fact that much Elizabethan bird poetry is constrained by the conventions of traditional pastoral verse, with melodious birds 'singing madrigals to love-sick shepherds',[5] it is still possible to claim that it is 'touched with a new naturalism'.[6] This is primarily a naturalism of sound or 'voice', rather than a naturalism of appearance or behaviour, but it does bring a new realism to the representation and evocation of bird song, and is especially concerned to convey the distinctive sounds made by different species. Touches of Elizabethan realism are to be found most impressively in the work of Michael Drayton, who, while drawing upon the birds of tradition and sometimes reverting to medieval conceptions, also introduces birds that were not part of tradition, and, moreover, sometimes treats them naturalistically rather than conventionally. In one passage in his long topographical poem *Poly-Olbion* (1612; 1622), he describes the movement of a large flocks of ducks over a fen, and also provides brief glimpses of individual species and specimens, including the mallard, teal, widgeon, and dabchick: 'The diving dabchick here among the rest you see, / Now up, now down again, that hard it is to prove, / Whether under water most it liveth, or above'.[7]

Munsterberg argues that the eighteenth century further narrowed the gap between realistic description and the traditional conventions and stereotypes surrounding birds. The poets of the period opted to use only such conventions as came closest to representing or suggesting the birds of nature, and thus they effectively 'trimmed the birds of tradition to more reasonable shapes'.[8] An older symbolism was retained but in a scaled-down way, and with recourse to a more naturalistic language of characterisation. The nightingale still features, for example, but without always having to press her breast against a thorn in order to make her singing more doleful – one of the traditional beliefs about the behaviour of the bird. The halcyon no longer magically calms the waves, but simply 'becomes the blue-coloured bird of peaceful summer rivers',[9] while the pelican disappears from view altogether, indicative of the recognition that it is not in fact a British bird. At the same time, the lark is moved into a position of prominence, functioning as a model of eighteenth-century simplicity, elegance and modesty of charm. Munsterberg identifies James Thomson's long poem, *The Seasons* (1730; 1744), as containing the most realistic bird poetry of the period, despite the generally artificial tenor of his language. In several sections of the poem, Thomson writes descriptively about birds, without recourse to conventional beliefs or associations. Munsterberg concludes: 'Thomson's birds do not stand for anything else. They are themselves, immersed in activities that have nothing to do with man.'[10] A new ornithological democracy is also in evidence in Thomson's poem. While the nightingale features in the section on spring, so also does a whole chorus of more 'unconventional' birds, including the jay, rook and jackdaw, whose notes, harsh when heard in isolation, 'Aid the full concert; while the stock-dove breathes / A melancholy murmur through the whole.'[11]

In the next century, the Romantic poets display a more accurate knowledge of birds, though the real bird is often just the starting point to a flight of poetic reflection or fancifulness. For the realist, the natural object will always be the end point of a description or evocation, but for the Romantic 'it is a beginning, an opening, an entrance to his own experience'.[12] This is most obvious in the case of Keats and Shelley. Despite the fact that 'Ode to a Nightingale' is one of Keats's most famous poems, which in turn adds to the fame of the bird itself, the poem is not for the most part about the bird of the title, but rather about the poet's emotional and imaginative response to the bird's presence. Moreover, Keats leans heavily on conventional knowledge of the bird, especially its association with singing of an ethereal, uplifting kind. The same kind of point may be made about Shelley's use of the skylark. Having 'conceded' to the bird that he does not know what sort of being it really is – 'What thou art we know not' – Shelly launches into a series of extravagant similes, the better to pursue the elusive essence of the 'blithe spirit' that is the skylark. From a naturalistic point of view, this only takes him further away from the bird of nature – which does not mean that the resultant verse is without great poetic merit, or that Keats, Shelley and the Romantics did not make a significant contribution to the history of bird poetry. In one of her most original and revealing remarks on Romantic bird poetry, Munsterberg claims that in Romantic verse, 'the conventions are so enlarged, so enriched, so deepened, that they are utterly transformed, as if the stereotypes had been projected through a magic lantern'.[13]

The transformation of stereotypes may produce intriguing poetic effects, but it does not give us naturalistic truth. It is not until we enter the work and the mental world of John Clare (1793-1864) that a new standard of naturalism is reached. Like no other poet before him, Clare cuts through the conventions, symbolisms and associations surrounding and ultimately obscuring birds, and draws entirely on his own experience and close observation, frequently writing about 'new' birds – that is, birds that had not been part of poetic tradition. We soon see that there is a close link between the revelatory clarity and precision of his descriptive language and his deliberate departure from the diffuse poetic diction of other nature poets. As Munsterberg puts it, 'Clare saw nature in sharp particulars, and he tried to translate them as exactly as possible into words'.[14] He is, however, no passive observer, letting nature get to him, even 'ambush' him, as could be said to be the case with Wordsworth; rather, he searches, hunts, crawls on all fours, the better to see what is happening in the fields, heaths, hedges, woods, and undergrowth. Where the Romantics tended to transform the birds of their inspiration into blithe spirits and birds that never were, Clare simply gives expression to what he so carefully – and so caringly – observes. One significant difference between Clare and the Romantic poets is the frequency with which he writes about the most 'lowly' element of the bird world, namely, the nest, which he often describes in language that is at once exact and lyrical, as in these lines (which retain the irregular spelling and punctuation of the original) from 'The Thrush's Nest':

> How true she warped the moss to form her nest
> And modelled it within with wood and clay
> And bye and bye like heath bells gilt with dew
> There lay her shining eggs as bright as flowers
> Ink-spotted over shells of greeny blue
> And there I witness in the summer hours
> A brood of natures minstrels chirp and fly
> Glad as the sunshine and the laughing sky[15]

Victorian poetry reveals both Romantic and realistic elements, according to Munsterberg, sometimes merging or compounding them into a moderate middle ground. There are no John Clares in the period, yet an impressive level of realism is maintained. There is a steady erosion of the 'bird traditions'; and the only conventions that remain in place are those that are reasonably realistic, such as the cuckoo standardly hailed as the herald of spring. More and more minor or previously unsung birds begin to have their day in the sun. By the time we get to the modern period, we find a new egalitarianism about birds and an intensification of Victorian individualism in which 'fragmented realistic impressions, often vivid and sharp, are combined with complex personal reactions'.[16]

While Munsterberg's account of the evolution of British bird poetry is for the most part wonderfully enlightening, it does lean towards a progressivist assumption that is open to question, especially with regard to the 'placing' of John Clare. The progression that is strongly hinted at in her introduction is a progression away from conventionalism and symbolism towards objective realism, with Clare seen not only as a mould-breaker but also as bringing to a head – and ultimately trumping

Swift   illustration courtesy of Michael O'Clery

Skylark

Nightingale   illustration courtesy of Michael O'Clery

Kestrel

illustration courtesy of Michael O'Clery

Cuckoo   illustration courtesy of Michael O'Clery

Hummingbird   illustration courtesy of Michael O'Clery

Corncrake

illustration courtesy of Michael O'Clery

Blackbird

illustration courtesy of Michael O'Clery
www.birdsireland.com/oclery.html

– the occasional or incidental gestures towards realism of a small number of earlier poets. His perceived achievement is not only to reject earlier conventional and symbolic treatments of birds, but also to reach a level of realism that has been taken up and moderated by later poets, beginning with the Victorians. It is this suggestion that there has been in English poetry a fitfully emergent impulse towards a realistic bird poetry, which finally came to a head in the work of John Clare, and was subsequently taken in different directions by later poets, that is to some degree questionable. We can readily agree that Clare is a nature poet *par excellence*, judged by realistic or naturalistic criteria, and that he sets the standard for all subsequent attempts at realistic writing about birds, other animals, and nature in general. I wish to argue, however, that Clare's poetry was not necessarily the revolutionary breakthrough that is suggested by Munsterberg, as if the spell of conventionalism, symbolism and other kinds of associative human thinking around birds was lifted forever – as if, in other words, Clare has had an effective and lasting influence on all subsequent nature poets. My argument will be that, while Clare is indeed a standard bearer for all subsequent nature poets, he is also in an important sense unique or *sui generis*.

I want to begin by dwelling on some of the best bird poems that appeared after Clare's time, beginning with Thomas Hardy's two poems, 'The Darkling Thrush' and 'The Selfsame Song', Gerard Manley Hopkins's 'The Windhover', and W B Yeats's 'The Wild Swans at Coole' – all in the Munsterberg anthology. We should soon see that these poems do not remind us very much of the naturalism of John Clare, despite being very fine bird poems in their own right. Their treatment of birds is sometimes as associative, even as conventional and as symbolic, as that in the work of poets before Clare. Hardy was, by his own admission not particularly interested in nature *per se*, as is clearly indicated in his remark that 'an object or mark raised or made by man on a scene is worth ten times any such formed by unconscious Nature'.[17] While there is no indulgence in conventional or archetypal associations in 'The Darkling Thrush', neither is there an attempt to describe the bird in appreciative and cumulative detail. Hardy assumes that the reader knows very well what a thrush is and how it looks and sounds. The most descriptive terms he uses – 'frail, gaunt, and small' – are sympathetically human ones, rather than strongly objective ones. What matters most to Hardy is the effect of the bird's surprisingly hopeful singing on himself and on anyone else who might care to listen:

> So little cause for carolings
>   Of such ecstatic sound
> Was written on terrestrial things
>   Afar or nigh around,

That I could think there trembled through
　　His happy good-night air
Some blessed Hope, whereof he knew
　　And I was unaware.[18]

In 'The Selfsame Song', the singing bird is not even named – an omission that Clare would not have countenanced – because, again, what matters to Hardy is the fact that the bird's singing prompts a poignant realisation about the perishability of all living things – including the singing bird and its song. Poetically, the bird is a means to an end, not an end in itself:

– But it's not the selfsame bird. –
No: perished to dust is he . . .
As also are those who heard
　　That song with me.[19]

Hopkins's windhover is not described at all, but is rather conjured up out of mimetic, evocative exhibitions of language that presuppose an existing familiarity with the bird in question, the kestrel. The reader with the best perceptual – indeed, conventional – knowledge of the appearance and flight pattern of the bird is the one best placed to appreciate Hopkins's own flights of language and his figurative condensations and rarefactions. The language is originally expressive rather than originally descriptive, and has more to do with the poet's perceptions and yearnings than with the bird itself. Moreover, it transpires that the poet is 'using' the bird to give expression to a religious feeling or intuition, and has not been seeking to do descriptive justice to the bird for its own natural sake. In the end, Hopkins abandons the bird, thematically speaking, when he realises and invokes the great gap that exists between the brute physical beauty of the bird and the superior, transcendent beauty of Christ, his 'chevalier'.

Poignant contrast between bird world and human world is also the theme of 'The Wild Swans at Coole', in which the seemingly unchanging reality of the birds is meaningfully set over against the changed and changing life of the poet. To the ruefully imaginative mind of the poet, the hearts of the birds have not grown old or weary, or less passionate, since he first heard the 'bell-beat of their wings' over his head nineteen autumns ago. But his own heart in the meantime has grown sore, and he is oppressed by change. Not only are the swans 'exploited' to give expression to a sense of time passing and life changing, but they are also spoken of in exaggerated and idealised terms – to the point, indeed, of paradox. On the one hand, they are partially humanised, insofar as they are seen as lovers, capable of passion and conquest; on the other, they are represented as lying outside or beyond the reach of the irresistible forces that pervade the changeable, mortal human world where the body ages and passion fades. In the case of both Hopkins and Yeats, we have before us some wonderful writing – but it is not wonderful for anything like the same reasons that the writing of John Clare is also wonderful.

What is true of Hopkins and Yeats is also true of a number of other twentieth-century poets who have written in earnest – that is to say, more than incidentally – about birds, without achieving the realism of John Clare, namely, Edward Thomas, D H Lawrence, and Ted Hughes. These poets are not represented in the Munsterberg anthology, but they are all well represented in the Armitage and Dee. (While the Armitage and Dee contains work by non-British as well as British and Irish poets, I am going to limit my comments here to the latter, with the exception of a reference at the end to a 'British' poem by Sylvia Plath). Edward Thomas is the only one whose work could be said to show the influence of Clare to any significant extent. The most Clare-like of his poems is 'Birds' Nests', which appears opposite Clare's poem of the same title in the anthology. The particular nest on which the poet dwells is not described as it looks in spring, but as it looks later in the year when it has been exposed and dislodged by autumn winds. The poet then makes an unClare-like admission:

> Since there's no need of eyes to see them with
> I cannot help a little shame
> That I missed most, even at eye's level, till
> The leaves blew off and made the seeing no game.[20]

Thomas's most impressive bird poems are those in which he reflects ultimately and poignantly on emotional human realities, as in 'She Dotes'. In this complex poem, a grieving woman sometimes laughs, sometimes cries at the fact that all the birds around her continue to sing and chatter to their hearts' content, despite the fact that her loved one has died. That there is craziness in her grief is suggested by her attempt to persuade herself that the birds are merely chiding her for thinking that death can divide her from her lover: 'And she has slept, trying to translate / The word the cuckoo cries to his mate / Over and over'.[21] At an even further remove from Clare's naturalism is 'The Unknown Bird', in which the poet recalls 'three lovely notes' that he heard one summer, soft and far off, as if he or the bird were in a dream: 'As if a cock crowed past the edge of the world'.[22] These notes – not known, he claims, to the naturalists – continue to bring him great lightness of heart whenever he remembers them. It is in poems such as this that Thomas's strengths are most in evidence, and not so much in the more Clare-like 'Birds' Nests'.

In the bird poems of D H Lawrence – three of which are contained in the Armitage and Dee anthology – we have a return to the enlargement and transformation of stereotypes that Munsterberg imputed to the Romantic poets, albeit with more touches of sublimity and terror than of beauty or charm. In 'Eagle in New Mexico', for example, we find Lawrence drawing upon the ancient belief that the eagle can stare at the sun, hence the references throughout the poem to 'scorched breast', 'sun-breaster', 'burnt dark feathers', 'feathers still fire-rusted' and 'fiery bird of prey'. The eagle is addressed as fierce and bloodthirsty: 'When you pick the smoky red heart from a rabbit or a light-blooded bird / Do you lift it to the sun, as the Aztec priests used to lift red hearts of men?'[23] In the end, Lawrence differs from his Romantic predecessors in refusing to celebrate or sing the praises of his chosen bird, a bird of prey. His responsiveness to the darker, more sublime aspects of birds is not confined, however, to birds of prey. Even the hummingbird can send the poet's imagination into a primitively fearful spin:

> I can imagine, in some otherworld
> Primeval-dumb, far back
> In that most awful stillness, that only gasped and hummed,
> Humming-birds raced down the avenues.[24]

In a very short time, the poet's imagination has magnified the little bird out of all proportion to its natural dimensions, imagining it to have 'flashed ahead of creation', and even to have been 'a jabbing, terrifying monster'. Such darkly sublime imagining is so far removed from the original bird of nature that it bears in the end no resemblance at all to the humbler, less visionary sorts of characterisations that we associate with the naturalism of John Clare.

Something of Lawrence's dark sublime resurfaces in the bird poetry of Ted Hughes, author of one of the most notorious bird poems of the modern period, namely, *Crow*. This extraordinary work is for the most part a feat of purely imaginative and associative thinking, and contains little in the way of close, sympathetic observation. Crow is an imaginary, quasi-mythical entity, a fulsomely symbolic scapegoat that is also at the same time a creature of human fears, horrors, and impulses. It is the product of a human imagination working very much on the far side, as well as on the dark side, of things. Such an imagination is very different from, say, the Wordsworthian imagination or the naturalistic imagination – the kind of imagination that does its best work on the near side of things, illuminating, magnifying or otherwise reconceiving things, but never displacing them. The Hughesian imagination, as we find it at work in *Crow*, shows little or no allegiance to the natural objects that are alluded to in the poem, least of all to the common-or-garden crow. *Crow* is all hectic, frenzied connotation, containing little in the way of denotative truth. The nearest that Crow comes to the crow of nature is perhaps in the section entitled 'Crow and the Birds' – the section reprinted in the Armitage and Dee anthology – where he is contrasted with a litany of other birds, all of which are more or less delicately represented: 'Crow spraddled head-down in the beach-garbage, guzzling a dropped ice-cream.'[25] But even in this 'realistic' line, the description is shot through with anthropomorphic judgment. In many other sections of *Crow*, Crow is the target of a good deal of baleful imagining and fabulously scornful myth-mongering. Nothing could be further removed from the joyfully lyrical naturalism of John Clare than Ted Hughes's *Crow*.

In some of his other poems, Hughes comes closer to lyrically speaking the truth about birds, especially in 'Skylarks' and 'Swifts', where the sounds and flight patterns of the birds are tracked and shadowed in the formal features – the line-breaks, stanza-breaks, and shifting rhythms – of the poems themselves, as well as in the constant semantic 'striving' of the language of evocation. But even in these poems, a surprising level of negatively anthropomorphic judgment enters in:

Crueller than owl or eagle

A towered bird, shot through the crested head
With the command, Not die

But climb

Climb

Sing

Obedient as to death a dead thing.[26]

'Obedient as to death a dead thing'! And this said of the skylark! In a later stanza, the skylarks are described as 'Squealing and gibbering and cursing // [...] The mad earth's missionaries.' The swifts are not as harshly judged, though they too are linked to death:

A bolas of three or four wire screams
Jockeying across each other
On their switchback wheel of death.[27]

Even when the poet reports burying a fledgling swift that he tried, unsuccessfully, to get to fly, he cannot seem to resist betraying in the end a bleakish human judgment:

                    Finally burial
For the husk
Of my little Apollo –

The charred scream
Folded in its huge power.[28]

What Munsterberg says of the treatment of birds in earlier poetry – that
birds are 'accessories to the human scene' – can also be said of a great
deal of more recent poetry, including much of the poetry written after
John Clare. It can be said of Hughes's best-known bird poem, 'Hawk
Roosting', in which anthropomorphic judgment once more comes
powerfully into play. Perhaps more than any other modern bird poem,
'Hawk Roosting' labours under a paradox that besets any poet who
attempts to write about a non-human form of life, while at the same
time giving implicit expression to human attitudes and emotions. The
poet regards the hawk as the compacted essence of Darwinian nature,
red in beak and claw, devoid of all the sympathies of which human
beings are capable – as if human sympathies, belated in evolutionary
terms, are not quite as real as the older, more bloody-minded instincts of
the bird of prey. The hawk enjoys 'no falsifying dream'; it kills where it
pleases; it needs no argument to support its 'right', which is to follow the
path of its flight 'Through the bones of the living'. But for all its brutal,
inhuman imputation, this tough-minded conception of the hawk is all
human perception and projection, all brilliant poetic conceit, and is not
based on any real understanding – impossible, in any case – of what it is
like to be a hawk, roosting or otherwise. The hawk is not represented but
rather made to represent an idea, namely, the idea of an overseeing, over-
bearing, fascistically manipulative human mentality. The hawk, like
Crow, is misrepresented, we might say. At the very least, the bird of
nature is lost in the antics, linguistic and conceptual, of the poet's
imagination. It is, by contrast, a radically important feature of Clare's
naturalism that it is not judgmental in the way that Hughes's poetry is,
nor is it ever prepared to 'frame', for poetic effect, any non-human
creature – even a bird of prey. Clare does not assume that a bloody-minded
conception of a bird or animal is necessarily the one that will take us
closer to grasping its nature.

    This is not to say that Clare's poetry is mere versified ornithology.
Munsterberg tends to separate out Clare's supposedly descriptive writing
from his supposedly personal responses to the observed details of nature.
But such a clear duality does not exist in Clare's poetry. At one point,
Munsterberg herself suggests a more integrated conception of his
achievement. She writes that his work 'is charged with a kind of wonder
and joy, as if he were saying: Look! This *is*, this is *true!*'[29] It is arguable

that all of his nature poetry is charged to varying degrees with this joy of observation. The freshness, sharpness, and vividness that Munsterberg attributes to Clare's exactitude of description might just as well be attributed to the originally joyful nature of his observation. It is not as if he begins by making factual observations, and then sometimes follows these with a joyful response, which later makes its way into some poems, or into some parts of some poems. Rather, joy is almost always present to greater or lesser degrees, and it is this continual joy of observation that comes to express itself in such vividness of expression, exactitude and idiosyncrasy of word-choice, and plenitude of detail. This joy is different from that of the Romantic poets, since it remains close to the object of its causation, and does not soar away from it into either the ebullient, presumptive visions of, say, Shelley or the bleaker but equally presumptive visions of Ted Hughes. Much of the joy experienced and expressed by Clare is felt in the process of discovery, in learning more and more of the birds he observes. His subjectivity, as expressed in the poems, is not a Keatsian, Shelleyan, or even a Wordsworthian subjectivity, but one that is informed at every turn by facets of the thing itself, rather than by any notions, beliefs, moral lessons, myths or 'revelations' brought to mind by the experience of it.

It could be said in criticism of Clare that his determination to have a joyful response to nature means that he ends up avoiding the harsher truths about birds and animals in general, especially the birds and beasts of prey – the very ones that are so graphically represented in the work of Lawrence, Hughes and others. When violence features in Clare's work, it tends to be perpetrated by human beings rather than by birds or beasts of prey. Even when he does write about a bird of prey, as in 'The Puddock's Nest', he ends by noting the fact that the young birds are sometimes captured by the schoolboy who 'takes them home and often cuts their wing / And ties them in the garden with a string'.[30] In Clare's defence, it might be said that the very idea of harsher truths about birds is a question-begging one to begin with, since it already implies a projection of human values into the world of bird and animal behaviour – a world that the human sensibility and imagination cannot easily, if ever, breach. Clare often alludes to the ways in which human actions and attitudes impinge, sometimes destructively, on the life of birds and animals, and he might justify the resolutely joyful nature of his observations by offering them as a way of righting the balance of relations between the human and non-human worlds. His joyfulness is not any kind of Romantic self-indulgence – it is an exercise, at the level of heartfelt attitude, in restorative justice. If his disposition towards joyfulness of observation does indeed prevent him turning his attention to the fiercer birds of prey, then so be it. The limits here are not set by the poet's capacity to observe but by his determination to avoid the kind of 'persecution' of the bird world that has been a feature, historically, of the unequal relationship between the human and non-human worlds.

It is arguable, then, that John Clare has not been a pivotal influence in the evolution of a realistic or naturalistic tradition of bird poetry. He is rarer than that. He is, we want to reiterate, *sui generis*. Certainly, there was no one before him who achieved his level of lyrical naturalism, except in occasional interludes and passing glimpses – including the delightful glimpses contained in the anonymous Old Irish poems that have come to be known as 'The Scribe in the Woods', 'The Blackbird by Belfast Loch', and 'The Blackbird Calling from the Willow'.[31] But neither is there anyone who came after him who could be said to have carried forward, in a consistent and sustained way, the mantle of joyful observation of birds. There is no British – or Irish – tradition of naturalistic bird poetry, within which Clare could be said to hold a dominantly influential position. This is not to say that non-naturalistic bird poetry is not of great continued interest. Of course it is. Many of us would not be without the bird poems of Hardy, Thomas, Lawrence, or Hughes, just as we would not be without the earlier bird poems of the Romantics. It is to say only that John Clare stands alone, without equal, without successor. There are also, of course, individual poets who sometimes write fine individual poems that come close, or measure up on their own terms, to Clare's lyrical naturalism. The Armitage and Dee anthology contains a number of such poems, including Gillian Clarke's 'Curlew', John Hewitt's 'First Corncrake', Philip Larkin's 'Pigeons', Norman MacCaig's 'A Voice of Summer', and Sylvia Plath's 'Pheasants', but the relative rarity of such poems only serves to confirm the singular achievement of the singular John Clare.

References

1 Mike Mockler (ed.), *Flights of Imagination* (Poole: Blanford Press, 1982), p. 9.

2 Ibid., p. 8.

3 Ibid., p. 10.

4 Peggy Munsterberg (ed.), *The Penguin Book of Bird Poetry* (London: Allen Lane, 1982), p. 35.

5 Ibid., p. 46.

6 Ibid., p. 50.

7 Ibid., p, 187. The text has been modernised by Munsterberg.

8 Ibid., p. 58.

9 Ibid., p. 57.

10 Ibid., p. 62.

11 Ibid., p. 229.

12 Ibid., p. 70.

13 Ibid., p. 71.

14 Ibid., p. 74.

15 Eric Robinson and David Powell (eds) *John Clare: Major Works* (Oxford University Press, 2004), p. 210.

16 Ibid., p. 98.

17 Florence Emily Hardy, *The Life of Thomas Hardy* (London: Macmillan and Co., 1962), p. 116.

18 Peggy Munsterberg (ed.), *The Penguin Book of Bird Poetry*, p. 310.

19 Ibid., p. 310.

20 Simon Armitage and Tim Dee (eds), *The Poetry of Birds* (London: Penguin Books, 2009), p. 212.

21 Ibid., p. 184.

22 Ibid., p. 278.

23 D H Lawrence, *Birds, Beasts and Flowers* (Boston: Black Sparrow Press, 2008), p. 107.

24 Simon Armitage and Tim Dee (eds) *The Poetry of Birds*, p. 130.

25 Ibid., p. 231.

26 Ibid., p. 148.

27 Ibid., p. 128.

28 Ibid., p.129.

29 Peggy Munsterberg (ed.), *The Penguin Book of Bird Poetry*, p. 76.

30 Eric Robinson and David Powell (eds) *John Clare: Major Works*, p. 272.

31 See Gerard Murphy (ed.), *Early Irish Lyrics* (Oxford University Press, 1956), pp. 5, 7.

Rae Howells

PERIOD

His words are like bees,
I stand there, and withstand them,
The storm of them, already bleeding –
And then, for his pleasure, stung. They are so loud, angry

Such fierce things, a sentence
That now I always carry:
I could not hold the baby.
I could not carry the baby.

He doesn't know it but
I baptise his words
With pints of my blood. I am a warrior,
Strung about with the teeth of enemies.

But he says his blithe speech
And I stand there, my ugly womb
The barrenness of me
Feeling raw as a peeled fruit

Nobody's muse – the coffin
Of my belly wagging open
Trailing its full stop
Snagged on the competition

Of my hard day's work,
Measured against the men's
And found wanting. And then too
Wanting in motherhood:

The working mother, broken.
Punctuation, that's all I am good for:
Failure and a little proofreading.
Just stay in your place: period.

Well none of that's for me.
I spell out my words for myself,
And also for my daughter.
Each interval is a space, a breath, a strength.

Rae Howells

THE DUNNS
 – after 'Adlestrop', by Edward Thomas

Yes, I remember the Dunns –
The pun of that pained twist of death
Where all that could be done was done
Despairingly. But was not enough.

Days we lay, curled like prawns in the arms
Of a brown leather sofa, crying for
A death we knew would come
As sure as rain, but hoped would not.

It was a quick shove in the end,
A cut and push of muscles and slipped
Mess, like a bag of soft black velvet
Left out in the wet too long, and lost.

The curl of wax in the water was the only sign
Black folding back to black.
The clouds parted for us, then,
And we saw a crowd of shining stars, like tiny hands.

Mark Mullee

THE DETAILS

Everyone who wasn't driving was walking.
Some lingered at shop windows, some to tie their laces,
Others waited for the light to change, red in their faces.

Everyone who wasn't working was taking it easy.
On the sidewalk, in the sunshine, a man at a table for two
Was delighted to see asparagus soup back on the menu.

Everyone who wasn't talking was moving their lips.
In the bookshop across the street, a girl perused a novel
In which the protagonist yearns for her father's approval.

Everyone who wasn't reading was getting things done.
I was in the barbershop, getting a straight shave,
When the shop shook and I felt the nick of the blade.

Some forget the details, but all remember the sound –
A boom and then a rattle, then the many car alarms,
And everyone who wasn't standing was lying down.

Mark Mullee

RESERVATIONS AT A BRAZILIAN STEAKHOUSE

In the spirit of a gaucho practised in the art
of deftly throwing his pair of bolas
around the ankles of a runaway steer,
this waiter throws his arms around my stomach,
and with the quick pump of the Heimlich,
to the sound of strangers erupting in cheer,
manages to dislodge the bolus
stuck there like a half-chewed heart.

Marina Tsvetaeva

'I DON'T REMEMBER WHO IT WAS'

I don't remember who it was
pinned that flower to my coat.
My yearning for passion, sadness
and death is not yet quenched.

I hear it in a cello's tones,
in creaking doors, in clinking
glasses and in jingling spurs,
in cries from evening trains,

when shots ring out during the hunt
or carriage bells pass by –
your repeated summons to me,
all you I did not love!

One consolation still remains:
I'm waiting for the man
who'll understand the thing I need
and shoot me down, point-blank.

22 October 1915

– translated by **Christopher Whyte**

Marina Tsvetaeva

'HELL'S WHERE WE'RE BOUND FOR, GORGEOUS SISTERS'

Hell's where we're bound for, gorgeous sisters,
we will be forced to drink black pitch,
who sang the praises of the Lord
straining our voices till they broke!

We who would never bend at night
over spinning-wheels or cradles,
unsteady boats will transport us
huddled in our flapping cloaks.

Dressed from the moment we got up
in thin, delicate Chinese silks,
around the robbers' bonfire we
led choruses from paradise.

Hopeless when it came to sewing –
this way, that way, nothing worked! –
lording it over the whole world,
dancing and playing on the flute,

squinting at the constellations
in rags that barely covered us,
carousing and promenading
through the islands of the skies,

strolling beneath a flood of stars
through the orchards of paradise –
darling girls, beloved sisters,
we shall all end up in Hell.

November 1915

– translated by **Christopher Whyte**

Marina Tsvetaeva

'A TIME WILL COME, RIVAL OF MINE...'

A time will come, rival of mine, when I'll
pay you a visit on a moonlit night,
while frogs can be heard wailing from the pond,
and pity drives women out of their minds.

The palpitation of your jealous eyelids
and eyelashes will move me to compassion,
and I'll insist I'm not a human creature,
merely a dream that's being dreamt by you.

And I'll implore you: 'Comfort me! Comfort me!
Somebody's driving nails into my heart!'
I'll tell you that the evening's cool, that far
above my head the stars are burning hot.

8 September 1916

– translated by **Christopher Whyte**

Fran Brearton

POETRY AND FORGETTING: ON HEWITT'S 'NEITHER AN ELEGY NOR
A MANIFESTO'

This is an abridged version of the talk given by Dr Brearton on 25 July 2011 in the
Market Place Theatre and Arts Centre, Armagh, as part of the 24th John Hewitt
International Summer School.

> Bear in mind these dead:
> I can find no plainer words.
> I dare not risk using
> that loaded word, Remember...[1]

John Hewitt's early 1970s poem, 'Neither an Elegy nor a Manifesto' is a
poem about the politics of memory and memorialising, and an
embodiment of them; it also has, or courts, the quality of being forgettable,
even as it wants to make itself heard. It is, therefore, a poem of paradox,
both iconic and iconoclastic, putting in mind what it strives to avoid,
setting itself up for failure. In these opening lines, 'Remember' is a 'loaded'
word in the sense of being freighted, burdened with historical and
political pressures (through exhortations to remember 1690, 1798, 1916) in
a way which needs no further explication here. To remember the dead
makes no difference to the dead; how or whether they are remembered
may make all the difference to the living. To remember, in one
definition, is to recall the memory of a person or event with feeling or
intention. So the word can be, as Hewitt knows, a dangerous one – loaded,
like a gun perhaps, and something that may discharge itself in violence.

   Yet it's loaded in another way too, since remembering carries within
it, exists only on the basis of, forgetting. To remember is 'not to forget';
to forget is 'to lose remembrance of'. As Derek Mahon puts it in the early
poem 'Spring in Belfast': 'Once more, as before, I remember not to
forget.' Remembering and forgetting are inseparable and they are often
both necessary. If the twentieth century was a century obsessed with
remembrance in a way no other has been, it is also the case, as Adrian
Forty notes, that 'forgetting has, in a manner of speaking, been *the* problem
of the twentieth century. ... In post-war Europe, the ability to forget has
been put to the most severe test. The relative stability of Western Europe
since 1945 has in part been due to a colossal act of collective, consensual
forgetting...'.[2]

   The need to remember, and the need to forget, are held in tension –
in politics, in society, in the individual too. They're held in particular

tension in John Hewitt's aesthetic, and manifest themselves there in ways that are highly distinctive. That might be illuminated by thinking about some of the problems of memorialising as they've emerged through two world wars – notably the concept of the memorial, and of the anti-memorial – and to map these onto the oddness one finds in Hewitt of the poem in tension with a kind of (forgettable) anti-poem.

War memorials constructed in the aftermath of World War I generally work on the principle that something solid is built to preserve, for all time, what has been lost: 'Lest we Forget'. A permanent presence reminds us of a permanent absence. The solidity and durability of some war memorials seems to embody the sentiment inscribed on them. One example might be the Cenotaph, another the Stone of Remembrance placed in the British military cemeteries in France and Belgium and inscribed with the words: 'Their Name Liveth For Evermore'. They are large, solid, stone objects, whose physical form is implicated in what they try to do – resist forgetting. They work on the principle that 'memories, formed in the mind, can be transferred to solid material objects, which can come to stand for memories and, by virtue of their durability, either prolong or preserve them indefinitely beyond their purely mental existence'.[3]

Yet as time goes by are such memorials really *seen*? They become almost invisible, despite their size, their solidity. That may be one reason to doubt the relation between objects and memory; another, post-1945, as Forty points out, 'has been brought about by the difficulties of remembrance of the Holocaust, and the realisation that conventional memorial practices were inadequate and inappropriate to the task.'[4] The problem is one that Adorno identified in 1962. To write lyric poetry after Auschwitz, he said, is barbaric; yet, as he went on to say, 'literature must resist this verdict'. He identifies a paradox, an aporia, in that 'suffering demands the continued existence of art while it still prohibits it':

> The so-called artistic representation of the sheer physical pain of people
> beaten to the ground by rifle butts contains, however remotely, the
> power to elicit enjoyment out of it. The moral of this art, not to forget
> for a single moment, slithers into the abyss of its opposite. The aesthetic
> principle of stylization … make[s] an unthinkable fate appear to have
> had some meaning; it is transfigured, something of its horror is
> removed. This alone does an injustice to the victims; yet no art which
> tried to evade them could stand upright before justice.[5]

It's also something Paul Muldoon identifies in relation to poetry and the Troubles in 1984: 'If you don't engage in it, you're an ostrich… If you do engage in it … you're on the make, almost, cashing in'.[6] Or, one might say, you're damned if you do, damned if you don't.

One response to the problem has been the emergence of a genre of anti-memorials, memorials that try to express the paradox of remembering and forgetting, aware of their own inadequacy, and perhaps even their own culpability (their potential, that is, to render the unthinkable 'thinkable' in a way which falsifies, and therefore effectively forgets, the experience they simultaneously purport to remember). Two such memorials, by the German artist Jochen Gerz, are self-conscious about the ways in which they are doomed to failure, doomed perhaps to be forgotten.

The first is the Hamburg Memorial against Fascism, described by Gerz as a counter-monument. Unveiled in 1986, it was an aluminium, lead-plated pillar, 12 metres high, 1 metre wide. Initially it looked much like traditional monuments. But it was transient and fluid, not permanent and fixed. People were invited to sign their names on it with a steel stylus. Each time 1 ½ metres of the pillar were covered with signatures, it was lowered into the ground – six or eight times in total – until it was sunk completely in 1993.

The second is the Place of the Invisible Monument in Saarbrücken, Germany. Between 1990-93, Gerz and his students, at first clandestinely, removed 2,146 cobble-stones from a town square, engraved on the underside of each the name of a (desecrated) Jewish cemetery in Germany before 1933, then replaced them with the inscription pressed into the ground, permanently hidden. It's an invisible monument, one to be 'walked over'.[7] Since any memorial can become almost absent and forgotten, part of the landscape that is no longer seen, a text that is 'unread', these counter-monuments are not acts of commemoration, but anti-monuments that commemorate forgetting to remember. They're a paradox, in that to trigger memory, they have to be remembered in advance of the fact; it is their absence that gives them a presence.

This might seem to take us a long way from Hewitt. But Hewitt, with his interest in, and understanding of, the world wars, and his own work in the field of preservation and memory, is remarkably attuned to some of the broader problems surrounding remembering and forgetting. Remember is a word he dares to use, if not often, then often enough to see a pattern emerge in the memory work his poems undertake:

> 'I wrestled with my father...then suddenly remembered who we were'
> ('Jacob and the Angel'); 'remembering that satin pouch of poems, / I
> clasp her bony hand' (My Grandmother's Garter'); 'remembering / they'll
> be outlasted by the marching stars / and...no man dare be too sure of
> anything' ('Sunset over Glenaan'); 'holding your tongue from quick
> comparisons; / remembering that you are a guest in the house' ('The
> Search'); 'if we remember when life first arose' ('Freehold').

'Remembering' is not negatively loaded in Hewitt's poems, it is a positive force. It is about, variously, remembering loved ones, the ordinary people who make up the tapestry of the poet's own personal history and who would otherwise be forgotten. It places necessary checks and balances on one's own behaviour (the opposite of 'forgetting oneself'). It is about an awareness of man's place in the natural (or spiritual) world –an avoidance of hubris. His work thus exhibits, as we might expect, a fear of forgetting, of what he calls in 'The Municipal Gallery Revisited' 'the creeping haircracks of indifference'.

But this is only one side of a paradoxical coin. As Terence Brown writes, Hewitt 'understands the spectres that haunt and threaten his province and sets about the task of exorcism with a serious, intent concern', while at the same time he fulfils a less 'exalted duty' with 'quiet zeal' – the 'duty to record and celebrate the everyday life of a people – to save even "a little people" from oblivion'.[8] Or, one might say, he recognises the need to forget *and* the need to remember. For all the reiterations of the word remember in his work, we can set beside them another preoccupation too, found in those poems which step outside individual into collective memory and politicised identity, an anxiety about 'poisoned memory', about 'ways of hate' that are 'long-nurtured', in an island 'maimed by history'.[9] Where poisoned memory endures, the wound is kept green; the people are 'never checked' in the way that Hewitt's more positive forms of remembering would check behaviour. To dream, in 'The Dilemma', of 'unfettered thought', of a 'free' people is, in effect, to say people should also be free to forget, which also means free to remember differently.

These two preoccupations in Hewitt – with remembering, with forgetting – are not contradictory; they are necessarily intertwined. And they bring me back to 'Neither an Elegy nor a Manifesto', a poem which embodies the paradoxes of remembering and forgetting at the heart of much 'memory work' in the twentieth century.

An elegy remembers what is past, a manifesto anticipates a future: this poem is simultaneously neither and both. Its opening line, 'Bear in mind these dead' is followed with 'I can find no plainer words'. But 'bear in mind' is not a plain phrase. It means to keep in mind, to recall to mind; but also to suffer in one's mind perhaps, to carry a burden. And it has behind it the echo of bearing a coffin, of the dead literally carried with us. The line is monosyllabic; but it's not plain in terms of a clear, one-dimensional meaning. The 'hedge of dead bramble, heavy / with pathetic atomies', is an oblique war landscape of barbed wire and skeletons. The poem will not advocate prayer in the second stanza, since 'prayer in this green island / is tarnished with stale breath, / worn smooth and characterless / as an old flagstone'. '[T]arnished', that is, as if it were a physical object. The eschewal of failed strategies here recalls some of the conventional, worn, stone monuments, or bronze statues, with fading inscriptions, that no longer fulfil the purpose for which they were built.

There is an awareness , too, that conventional memorial practices cannot cope anymore: 'I might have recited a pitiful litany / of the names of all the dead: / but these could effectively be presented / only in small batches'. Yeats recites a litany of names in 'Easter 1916', one that is definitely not 'pitiful', either in the sense of being futile, or of evoking 'pity' (and Yeats was not a poet for whom 'pity' formed part of his world-view). Hewitt's poem is conscious of Yeats's great political elegy, but far removed from it in style and ambition. The dead of Hewitt's poem, who can only be presented in 'batches' (a sinister, rather clinical term in itself), literally cannot be 're-membered'. Re-membered, that is, in its archaic sense of putting things together again, reversing a dismembering, seeing them 'whole' or entire. The 'policeman dismembered / by the booby-trap in the car', gives us the only direct echo of, or 'companion' word for, 'Remember' in its opening stanza. The poem is, in terms of theme and content, self-consciously concerned with the politics of remembering and elegising, as well as apparently containing within it its own exhortation to remember ('Bear in mind…'). But it is more complicated than that too, in terms of its form, language, and style.

Yeats's 'Easter 1916' is one of the most memorable poems of the twentieth century, with its haunting refrain, and its superb utilisation of the ballad tradition to enhance its power. Refrains (as in 'A terrible beauty is born') intensify poetic memorability. The principle is not confined to poetry and poetic form. Alan Baddeley's study of human memory points out that 'there is a strong relationship between the imageability of a word and the ease with which it can be remembered'; that memories practised and rehearsed and retested are more likely to endure. And, of relevance to poetry too, he cites the case of Professor Aitken, who could 'recall to the first 1,000 decimal places the value of *pi*' (the ratio of any circle's circumference to its diameter). He did so by arranging the numbers in rows of 50, with ten groups of five in each row, and reading them in a particular rhythm, an almost incantatory style.[10] In a sense, one might say he made a poem out of *pi*, and that is how he remembered it.

Hewitt wilfully resists the poetic devices, the form and style that would render his poem memorable. 'Neither an Elegy nor a Manifesto' is in verse paragraphs, irregularly patterned – not an unmemorable thing in itself of course, but a notable refusal of the regular rhythms that characterise much of his poetry. It avoids rhyme. By the third verse, the diction has become profoundly anti-poetic, adopting or parodying the language of the 'manifesto' or the media: it over explains (the 'careful words'); it adopts scientific and legalistic discourse ('injunction', 'unaligned', 'propose'); the poem is almost ponderous in places ('these could effectively be presented'). The extreme point comes in the fourth verse with 'but do not differentiate between / those deliberately gunned-down / and those caught by unaddressed bullets: / such distinctions are not relevant'. The writing is prosaic in the extreme, dry and preachy. The style here is deliberately forgettable, in its refusal of mnemonic devices. Hewitt is more than capable of the memorable lyric, but largely avoids anything that would give this poem such lyric qualities. It is, therefore, in some ways, an anti-poem, like the anti-memorials erected in Germany in the 1980s and 1990s, a poem which refuses any easy terms on which it can be remembered, whilst also saying 'do not forget'. To recall Adorno, one can say this poem is also resistant to stylisation, aware of its ethical dilemma, scrupulous in its refusal to create a verbal icon.

Yet a poem that refuses what makes it a poem, must surely fail too. Hewitt can't write out of his text entirely those things which make it a work of art, that make artistic capital out of suffering – indeed, the poem cannot, if it is even to exist, do anything else. His words, he says, 'do not pound with drum-beats'. Yet if we look at the two lines which precede his prosaic instructions quoted above, they are: 'So I say only: Bear in mind / those men and lads killed in the streets'. Their rhythmical quality is incantatory; he uses octosyllabic, iambic tetrameter (the rhythm of Yeats's 'Easter 1916'); and with the introduction of the slightly archaic 'lads' he draws not on the plainest words, but on those most tellingly emotive (the language of elegy). His reaction against that lyricism is extreme perhaps, but it jars all the more in its resistance to stylisation *because* it follows on from its opposite. Avoiding Yeatsian refrain, the exhortation to 'bear in mind' nevertheless repeats itself five times in the poem. And the last line irresistibly draws to its close in a perfect iambic pentameter, the line that comes naturally to poetry in English, that imprints itself on the memory more than any other: 'but, at this moment, bear in mind these dead'.

It is an uneasy poem, a poem struggling with itself, with its own 'nature', with its own being *as* a poem. The work of art is created; but Hewitt is an iconoclast, who as he creates the artefact, the monument, also destroys it from within, sinks it into the ground, makes it invisible to the memory through his resistance to mnemonic devices. In a poem such as 'The Harvest Bow', Heaney does the opposite: he creates the icon. Heaney's harvest bow 'does not rust'; it is 'burnished' unlike Hewitt's 'tarnished' memory; it is presented as what it is not – a solid object which endures even beyond, say, the bronze statue, a conduit into the past, a trigger to memory: 'And if I spy into its golden loops / I see us walk between the railway slopes / Into an evening of long grass'. It is palpable, an object he can 'tell and finger'; a living breathing thing, 'still warm'. The harvest bow, like the poem itself, carries an awareness of its own vulnerability: it could be 'throwaway', or, the implication is, thrown away. It's a 'frail device'; but the sheer beauty of the imagery and diction, the perfection of form, the haunting quality of its rhythms, work against frailty to make this, perhaps in a more traditional and more familiar sense, the work of art which aspires to permanence.

Poems aren't memorials, of course, and the degree to which a poem is a tangible material object is a question for another day. But such is the nature of the medium, a poem can express complexities in a way that any memorial (even anti-memorial) struggles to achieve. Hewitt's poem, like any poem, is a finished and complete object; it has a kind of physical form, preserved on the page, in the book; but the process of reading is also one of discarding and forgetting, something that takes place over time. With each word and line we read there is a discarding of the one which preceded it. We don't experience a poem 'entire'; we experience it as something gradually disappearing, aware of its transience as much as its permanence. When Hewitt ends 'Neither an Elegy nor a Manifesto' with 'at this moment, bear in mind these dead', the moment, by the close of the line, is already gone. The poem doesn't just try to address a problem of remembering and forgetting that has haunted writers and artists in the twentieth century; it is itself that problem. It's unusual, perhaps, in embodying that problem so fully, and so self-consciously; its very uneasiness, its inability to resolve the contradictions on which it rests, make it one of the more interesting, and (ironically enough) more memorable poems he has written.

References

1 John Hewitt, 'Neither an Elegy nor a Manifesto', *Collected Poems*, ed. Frank Ormsby (Belfast: Blackstaff, 1991) pp.188-90.

2 'Introduction', *The Art of Forgetting*, ed. Adrian Forty and Susanne Kuchler (Oxford and New York: Berg, 1999) p. 7.

3 See Forty, *The Art of Forgetting*, p.2.

4 Ibid p.6.

5 Theodor Adorno, 'On Commitment' (1962), *Performing Arts Journal* 3.3 (Winter 1979) pp.60-61.

6 Quoted in Edna Longley, *Poetry in the Wars* (Newcastle: Bloodaxe, 1986) pp.12-13.

7 See http://memoryandjustice.org/site/monument-against-fascism/ and http://www.arttimesjournal.com/speakout/Oct_10_online_Callaghan/Oct_10_Callaghan.html

8 Terence Brown, *Northern Voices: Poets from Ulster* (Towata, N J: Rowman and Littlefield, 1975) pp.88, 90.

9 See Hewitt, 'An Irishman in Coventry' and 'An Ulsterman'.

10 See Alan D Baddeley, *Essentials of Human Memory* (Hove: Psychology Press, 1999) pp.23, 65, 118.

Bethan Kilfoil

SILHOUETTE

I'm in the kitchen of our childhood house
Looking up at my mother's silhouette
As she steadies herself beside the sink
Head down, and I know she's started to cry
Because her father's just died. 'You don't mind
About Taid, do you Mam?' I ask, my words

An anxious tug to make her turn, find words
To comfort us both in the empty house,
Her usual 'Don't worry, never mind';
But grief draws its relentless silhouette
Around her, and me, and I watch her cry,
The two of us, standing beside the sink.

But she's my mother and she will not sink
Into despair or depression – not words
She'll even countenance. No, she'll cry
A little, then start tidying the house,
With me in tow, obedient silhouette,
Both of us keeping busy because mind

Over matter is best. But my dream mind
Like hers, I know, drifts back to fall and sink
Into the warm world where the silhouette
Of Taid lingers – gentle man of few words,
I remember him up in the old house –
Ill in bed – they tell me I mustn't cry –

So, dressed in my nurse's kit, I don't cry,
I climb up, take his temperature, remind
Him to take my special tablets. The house
Is cheered, he laughs when I go to the sink
To wash my toy stethoscope, and have words
With the imaginary silhouette

Of stupid doctors. Then, Taid's silhouette
Driving the pick-up: because I don't cry
Or throw tantrums like the others, waste words
In chatter, I'm his pet: he doesn't mind
Taking me along. We watch the sun sink
Slowly, fast, behind the hills, the old house

A silhouette in the dusk, in my mind,
Try not to cry, Mam standing by the sink,
We share silent words in memory's house.

Jodie Hollander

VICTORIA PARK

I

May must be the worst month before death,
Mother, when the cold finally cracks –
and suddenly the flowers feel close.

It's that long knowing of the last;
the last chance to see the early morning
buds opening on horse-chestnuts;

to hear the wings of wild geese overhead;
and the last chance to witness the crocuses
repeating themselves over the new green land.

2

I'd rather be a curly-haired young dog
bounding through weeds, or else a meadow lark,
gliding clear above the silver birch trees.

Sometimes, I'd even rather be a child,
trampling barefoot through the dandelions;
chasing spores disappearing in the breeze.

Anything but this always *feeling* small.
How quickly I drop down to my knees and weep
for my heart, still unsprouted in the sunlight.

Denis Rigal

AUTUMN IN GRIGNAN
   – for Philippe Jaccottet

The gentle southern air still breathes each day
through yellow beeches as the light withdraws
from a blazing rustle of wild-cherry trees.
A great grey heron makes its careful way
darting now here, now there, its precise beak
for tiny creatures in the gathering mist.
The man, pausing beside the road, turns back
from a traditional ox-cart creaking past,
the axles of the same old local freight.
He puts a hand out to an orchard gate
(*Bonjour, monsieur Gauguin!*), points to a dark
second growth beneath apple branches twisted
by some mysterious pain and to the kindly
little valleys where there still persist
a little thyme yet for a little time,
some bare-field lavender in wilting rows
and grapes to gather after the first frost
that make this pale sweet wine, this quiet wine.

– translated by **Derek Mahon**

Richard Murphy

NOTES FOR SONNETS

Here are three chapters of a work in progress drawn from notebooks I kept in Killiney, County Dublin, while working on my sonnet sequence The Price of Stone *(Faber and Wake Forest, 1985). I had recently left Connemara, where I had lived for twenty years between Cleggan, Inishbofin, High Island, and Omey. Each chapter concludes with a sonnet of the same title – 'Miners' Hut', 'Pier Bar', and 'Wellington Testimonial'. I call the work in progress, amounting to thirty-three chapters, 'Transgressing into Poetry'.*

10 August 2011, Sri Lanka

MINERS' HUT

Mon 20 Sept 1982

The Omey strand of my 'Hexagon' sonnet is now closed. From that inward outlook it's a short if risky voyage across the sound of broken water to High Island, but the weather in my mind is fair.

Go back to the ocean side of the island, to the cliff edge where the ruins of the hermitage built by St Fechin in the seventh century lie sheltered in a dimple with a pond surrounded by rock. The last recorded hermit, St Gormgall, was buried there in 1018, and for the next eight hundred years the site was preserved by its sanctity as a place of pilgrimage. But in 1827 the little oratory and the corbelled cells and the underground passageways of those hermits were ransacked for stone to house miners working on the east side of the island facing the mainland. The mine was sunk for copper to relieve the debts of the great absentee landlord, Richard Martin of Ballynahinch, founder of the Royal Society for the Prevention of Cruelty to Animals. It yielded fool's gold.

The oratory at the centre of the hermitage was built for spiritual wealth, and the miners' hut for material. If I were to write the poem as if it were the present-day roofless oratory speaking, it might contain false nostalgia ... perhaps a solution would be to write a schizophrenic poem in which the speaker is a split person like myself, part roofless oratory, part restored miners' hut ... bits of his mind having been ransacked and divided long ago, carried away in creels on mules, splitting his holy soul from his greedy body ... this would be more interesting than two separate poems.

The destruction of the oratory and transfer of the stone to build the miners' hut is like a translation, but one that mutilates the original ... or like words given new meanings that obscure the old ... poetry can be creative archaeology that discovers and uses verbal roots ... it may find reverberations in the miners' hut ... but is not above the risk of succumbing to fashion or linguistic vandalism.

A sonnet version of the 'Miners' Hut' could address vandalism, but with the oratory in mind ... from the flagellating Celtic hermits to the extortionate mine owner, each looking for a different kind of gold, the distance is a mule-ride over cliff-paths, through wild flowers and birds' nests.

With six strong men on seven fine days in the summer of 1971, I restored one room of that hut as a den for eating, sleeping and writing notes for poems ... near a mineshaft on the edge of a cliff in extreme isolation ... in tune with the atonal cry of a seal on a rock in the belly of a cove ... random verbal responses to the mating and alarm calls of birds ... to the miniscule piping of rock-pipits in harebell crevices by day ... to the mewling and puking of storm-petrels on nests in the walls of the hut by night.

Built to help the founder keep a mistress in Bordeaux, the miners' hut, converted into a poem, should speak about cruelty to people as well as to animals, destruction of beautiful buildings, extinction of wildfowl, nest-robbers climbing cliffs to steal young falcons to sell to Saudi Arabian princes. All the ransacking, pillaging images or ideas I can remember may be subsumed in its structure, including my telephone conversations with a German investor in islands, who is putting his money into islands as a shelter from nuclear war.

I stole a carved stone cross from beside Brian Boru's well, when the island belonged to a sheep farmer, who didn't object when I told him. A year later, having bought the island, I returned the stone to annul my theft and purge my sacrilege.

Wild rabbits tame as in Eden, digging burrows in the oratory's earth floor ... the 'sieg heil' salute of the black-backed white-headed seagulls ... their sheen, swagger and panache as sentries on rocks above their nesting ground ... like stukas dive-bombing civilians ... lording it with beaks and talons.

A German buyer is coming by helicopter to look the island over ... the sea is rising to Wagnerian altitudes with wave after wave exploding against the cliffs ... seagulls lamenting a lost character, a broken oratory heart in the miners' hut ... listen for sounds to rise from the bottom of that shaft below sea level ... sounds of exploitation ... words like shaft and thrift ... your own subversive desire at the bottom of your mind to sell this poor place to grow rich.

Carved stone crosses ... corbelled stone beehive cells ... relics of artists who died in pursuit of salvation through prayer and fasting ... their faith

and hope, others' greed and impiety, everyone's fear and desperation ...
all should connect in the poem of a 'Miners' Hut' built of stone from a
demolished Oratory...

St Paul's Cathedral gobbled up by the Stock Exchange.

The miners had to climb down a slippery black rock carrying the ore to
load on to luggers ... the sea too rough for a boat to moor, no pier ... how
many miners lived in the hut? ... overcrowded, diseased or injured,
brutalised by hard work and hunger, abused by foremen ... insulted as
stupid or lazy ... cannibalised by employers at six pence a day for dangerous
work ... several men killed ... what did it matter to the masters if their
servants died of consumption or starved to death? ... their suffering, their
songs, their feuds, their drunkenness, their sacred and profane speech
would be forgotten ... once down that shaft a man might never come up
to fresh air ... misfortune kept him down below the seabed ... kept down
by ignorance and poverty, oppression and greed, sheer necessity.

The sonnet should speak about suffering ... self-inflicted like the
flagellations of hermits in damp stone cells ... or imposed on the poor,
like that of the miners down their shaft ... or accidental, like Tony's
football injury ... an event that caused his life to end like a flame blown
out by a gust of wind ... the miners praying to the Virgin Mary Mother
of God to save them ... digging below the seabed with pick and shovel,
bucket and rope, crowbar and pulley ... till the sea burst into the shaft.

Now storm-petrels nest in the ruins of their hut ... hundreds are caught
on summer nights in the nets of birdwatchers, who ring their legs with
identity tags and let them go on their way as far, perhaps, as the Cape of
Good Hope ... before they return to nest on the island where they were
hatched.

These notes are like a demolition site, all dislodged bits and pieces of a
structure on the way to being rebuilt. Remember the mantra that Yeats
used to recite to himself when confused: 'Hammer your thoughts into
unity'.

Often, not only in the past, but continually in the present, while I am
in the midst of writing a line, composing myself to pray in the oratory of
my mind, that oratory is demolished to provide the means to make
money. Adding the exercise of 'eloquence' to the place of 'prayer' in its
meaning, the word 'oratory' acquired a baroque carapace. With a split
mind, part oratory, part miners' hut, I go from seeking salvation in words
to breaking up the dedication which the art of eloquence demands, for an
easier gain from the work of other people ... all the wily ugly satanic
effort to control them in action whose purpose is profit to be spent on
comfort in another place or country.

Wed 22 Sept 1982

Consider separate poems for the Oratory and the Miners' Hut.

Divided mind ... anchoretic solitude or community of miners ... action or contemplation ... the conflict in myself ... the struggle that goes on and on ... how often have I sacrificed the oratory of thought for some new act that involved men building or excavating ... I sometimes felt happier as builder, man of action, sailor at the tiller of the *Ave Maria*, designer of the Hexagon and a shelter at the miners' hut ... than as a contemplative writing poetry ... yet some of these actions have resulted in poems.

The poem should resolve this dichotomy ... which splits me open when the telephone rings (as it might any moment now) and I wonder is it a call from an auctioneer to say that my offer (a bargain I cannot afford) for a cottage and ten acres of beach land at Claddaghduff has been accepted ... which would plunge me once again down a mine of activity and debt ... perhaps never to come up into the light of contemplation and poetry.

This is the moral of a poem that might emerge from the ruins of the miners' hut ... whose process of construction in pursuit of gold desecrated an oratory that hermits had built a thousand years earlier in quest of salvation ... that my process of restoring the hut as a shelter threatened to divert me from my quest of writing poetry there.

A form of active contemplation, or of contemplative action? Poetry as firm as stone but breathable as air. I need three rings of stone like the walls that used to surround the oratory on High Island to keep my thoughts from rambling ... like storm-petrels travelling over the ocean for most of the year, but returning to nest in holes under the scattered ruins of the hermitage ... I need to go back to being a hermit meditating in his cell ... to find among the notes scattered at random on the pages of this notebook a voice that may speak of its broken origin in a sonnet.

Sat 25 Sept 1982

Don't revise any more ... try a new poem of the first night spent on my own on High Island ... when I camped on the grass with my head on a cushion of thrift inside the outer wall of the hermitage ... or the second night when I pitched a tent inside the collapsed walls of the miners' hut ... woken by a storm-petrel fluttering against the tent as if it wanted to come in ... a poem of the building collapsed as it was when I first slept there ... and as it is now, abandoned and falling into dereliction again ... a poem as an image of myself ... of an oratory upbringing broken down for mundane purposes ... a plain style reforming the oratorical ... work ethic in wild decay ... the once holy ground of hermits ransacked by depredations of modernity.

Cross this path and you enter the dark.

MINERS' HUT

Unused in your desk drawer lies my brass key
To tongue-tied stonework, musky fossil tunes
You've locked away. Come back, not to unmask me
Word for word, but to make me sound in my ruins.

I rose from a desecration of corbelled cells
In holy cashels ringed by the flagellant sea:
Rock taken over by great black-backed gulls
Saluting each other *Sieg Heil*, claiming the sky.

Sink no more mineshafts to bring up fool's gold
With fever. You can't give every spall's lost face
A niche in the anchoretic oratory. Hold
My still-room as a rock-pipit's nesting place.

Bring oil to unseize my lock. The lode of ore
To smelt will sound like a fault: wheatear, shearwater.

Tues 28 Sept 1982

PIER BAR

4-13 Oct 1982

Tall grey barrack of rendered stone, three storeys high ... old as the
fishery dock that its white sash windows dominate ... watering-hole of
islanders weather-bound in Cleggan ... 'No boat will reach Bofin today ...
maybe not for a week ... with the seas going to the skies over the Stags ...
clouds ready to pour out of the heavens ... fill them up, Major!'
    That's what Major liked to hear ... pensioner of World War One ...
said to have returned from Mesopotamia with his back bent in the shape
of a curragh ... might not be true ... others say he started to bend his back
after the war in order to gain a British army pension ... married a teacher
and bought the Pier Bar for next to nothing ... previous owner out of
luck ... the fool had thrown a customer's fishing nets that were drying on
the Pier Bar fence into the sea.
    A former sergeant major, Major could bark orders ... he didn't like to
hear a carpenter whine, 'I'll fix your door-lock now in a minute, but give
me time' ... there was plenty of time in those days ... saving it got you
nowhere unless to England or America ... he ran the bar with his daughter,
who adored Dada so much that she never got married ... her tongue
could sting a drunk man like a wasp ... sweet as honey to a tourist.
    Trammel nets hung from the ceiling ... fishermen, when there were
fish, would squander money here ... boys and old men, heroes of tiller
and foredeck ... seldom a woman, unless a tourist, entered the bar ...
mothers and wives, sisters and daughters, waited at home for father or
brother or son to return from the sea or the pub ... families often deprived
if not bereaved ... Major, like a grizzled old bird of prey perched on a
barstool, kept a calculating eye on the boats landing people or fish on the
pier ... counting the boxes brought up from the *St John*, a small converted
hooker in which he owned a share.
    But mostly the pier was idle ... worm-eaten boats tied up in the dock
or abandoned to rot on the ground ... old men in the bar, deploring the
present, would glorify the past when thousands of barrels of salted herring
were sold in Cleggan to buyers from New York and St Petersburg ... when
forty nobbies, each crewed by seven men who were never afraid to go out,
would moor side by side at the pier ... good times that will never return,
now that foreign trawlers are allowed to suck up the fish with machines
like vacuum cleaners sweeping the ocean bed ... 'that can't be right'.
    Picture yourself disguised in a skipper's cap and yellow oilskins ...
sailing the *Ave Maria* from Cleggan pier to Inishbofin with a cargo of
anglers or trippers, day after day, summer weather permitting ... tourists
you indulge for seven hours on the boat in the sun, the wind and the spray,
on tide rips and shoals, reeling up pollock and mackerel on ten-feathered

jigs, becoming ankle deep in fish ... after their safe return imbued with the buoyancy of the sea, you join them in the Pier Bar for more entertainment ... with fish scales on your sleeves and boots ... a wad of fishy bank notes in your pocket.

Now I must try to distil a beery flow of words into a sonnet that gives a touch of bar-room pleasure ... a feeling for the danger, the love, and the intoxication of the sea ... as Dr Johnson wrote, 'The only end of writing is to enable the readers better to enjoy life, or better to endure it.'

I hated business, but got embroiled out of necessity and the wish to belong in that distant impoverished bleak corner of Connemara ... the whole question of who or what is a tourist, who or what is a native, used to be thrashed out in the Pier Bar ... truly I was born in the west of Ireland, though a drunk nationalist once accused me of having forged my birth certificate ... but I spoke like a tourist acting the part of a fisherman, becoming a voice for the fishermen ... and became, in the eyes of journalists, the Cleggan fisherman-poet ... a maritime figure attracting tourists to visit a rugged mythical land-and-seascape ... having written the copy and arranged for ten thousand brochures advertising the *Ave Maria* and the *True Light* to be printed at the Dolmen Press, publishers of my poetry ... earning as epitaph, 'Murphy put Cleggan and Inishbofin on the map'.

Trying to simplify the complexity of my life ... becoming a fisherman in order to write poetry from experience of the sea ... and wearing the mask of a fisherman to conceal the poet I wanted to prove myself to be ... much duplicity in living that split-level life ... and counter-cultural obstinacy in trying to revive the art of narrative poetry that Joyce was said to have killed, though he reinvented it, with *Ulysses*.

Bring the sea into the bar ... sea rhythms and sounds ... boat rhythms ... pressure and kick of the tiller under my arm and the hard roundness of its carved oak knob in my hand ... smell of oakum and tar ... name the boats ... *True Light* ... *St John* ... *Topaz* ... *Volunteer* ... *Star of the West* ... not for nostalgia ... there's more to say than to sigh about the sea at this crossing of a boundary in my life ... my literal transgressing.

'What time will the mail boat leave for Bofin?'
'When she's ready to go, if the weather is fit. You'd better be aboard, because she won't wait.'
'How will we know when she's ready?'
'You'll see her leaving the pier.'

That's how it was in Cleggan in the early nineteen-sixties ... the black pint of Guinness XX stout cost one shilling and four pence, when men earned twenty shillings equal to £1 a day on the roads, and the doctor charged the same to see a patient for ten minutes ... sawdust on the floor of the bar ... Major tapping a barrel ... cooper's art dying out ... Galway hookers almost extinct ... trying, how hard I tried, to revive the past ... digressing down backward lanes of hawthorn and hazelnut that might lead to glory or desolation ... in a moribund place with much talk of the dead ... 'he went fast, the poor man' ... 'better men than you tried that and failed, you're wasting your time' ... 'our plumber hadn't his new car a week but he'd taken his wife to seven funerals'.

'Fill them up, Major!' ... looking back at myself in the Pier Bar mirror, I seem determined to stay afloat the more they predicted 'Murphy will sink the *Ave Maria* and drown everybody aboard' ... as I nearly did ... trying to prove another kind of potency after my marriage had failed ... by succeeding in a difficult action of no importance but dare-devil risk ... wallowing in troughs of waves with a boy whose forceful courage saved me from sinking on the open sea ... a digression of joy in a life of digressions, as the sonnet may sing.

'Fill them up, Major!' ... again and again ... till the wind is shaking the door like an angry drunk locked out on a winter's night ... who above all were you hoping to see, coming from London, to turn the sad faces, sunk in their weather-bound torpor, bright with the prospect of fishing again, but Tony White? ... redeemer and prime entertainer ... who made you all feel better by his presence ... who, when talking to you in a crowd, without offending others who may have hoped to catch his eye, could make you feel his eyes on you alone.

PIER BAR

For donkey's years I've stood in lashing rain
Unbudgingly, casting a fish-hawk eye
On dock-tied hookers. How could we regain
Lost native custom tourist cash would buy?

Snug in my torporific trammelled air
Of a dream village roped to a lifeless quay,
I can help you play with an old craft, but your
Ten-feathered jigs will get fouled up at sea.

What brings you back to me, having said goodbye
To bull-head shillings in my hand-carved till,
Unless to greet, reflected through my dry
Distillery, the dead friend whose glass I fill?

Why drown so carefully with moss-hung chain
On sound moorings? Rig me. I'll entertain.

13 Oct 1982

WELLINGTON TESTIMONIAL

24 Nov – 8 Dec 1982

Finished revising 'Choir School' yesterday ... not a good poem, but I cannot make it better.

Try focusing on the Wellington Testimonial erected in Phoenix Park after Waterloo ... that cold expression of the ethos of a conqueror towering over an aisle of evergreen oaks ... before plunging back into turbid adolescence at the College in Berkshire ... never since leaving the college at the end of 1944 have I returned ... try both ways of netting the experience ... read family letters of the period ... and lives of Wellington by Sir Charles Petrie and Elizabeth Longford.

   The voice of an Old Wellingtonian ... standard English of an army officer ... a derogatory tone polished to command and make people cringe ... a voice that must never sound too clever by half, indicating unfitness to obey a stupid order without question ... the tone of Mrs Thatcher or her ministers talking down to the nationalists in Northern Ireland ... though I deplore that voice, sometimes erupting in anger unawares I use its cutting edge to make a sharp point.

   Entering Wellington College reluctantly at fifteen, instead of two years earlier ... placed in a house where a dozen hearty athletic boys of my age destined for careers in the forces were two years behind me in school ... and being Irish at a school founded for the sons of British officers ... and attracted by the naked bodies of boys I saw every morning when we had to strip and plunge one after the other into three cold baths summer and winter ... I turned inwards and rebelled by choosing to study nothing but English, History and Latin ... isolating myself in poetry and fiction from the library ... listening to classical music on records in the music rooms, to counter the crooning of Frank Sinatra from a radiogram at full volume penetrating every cubicle in our House ... no wonder the army boys mocked me.

   Yet there were times when I dreamed of becoming an officer in the Irish Guards, the Ninth Lancers, or the Black Watch, a Scottish kilted regiment ... of laying down my life to save my friend on a battlefield and win a posthumous VC ... how greatly this would have pleased my mother, three of whose admirers had been killed on the Western Front.

   A 'Wellington Testimonial' persona, in the mode of 'Folly', could speak about itself today ... as a monument isolated in a country and a century that have changed ... celebrating things or people that nobody remembers ... in a form now regarded as too rigid ... on behalf of a foreign power ... to commemorate a hero born in this country but who is reputed to have said, 'Because a man is born in a stable that does not make him a horse'.

Have all possible cadences been tried and exhausted in the sonnet? ... ask this question in the Wellington sonnets ... are you square-bashing in rhymed metrical verse ... constrained by the left right left right of the metre and the rhyme, the platoons of polished boots on parade?

Trace the connection, if there is one, between the sonnet as a love poem perfected by Petrarch and Shakespeare immortalising the beloved ... and the Wellington Testimonial, constructed to immortalise the saviour of the nation, the victor of Waterloo, the Iron Duke ... so precise, well-proportioned and banal ... but from some angles epical ... cold calculation put it there ... to stand high and indifferent over the Phoenix Park ... where Thomas Henry Burke and Lord Frederick Cavendish were murdered by the Invincibles in 1882 ... and where, last summer, a nurse who had gone to the park to sunbathe was tortured and murdered by a man later found to be staying in a Dalkey penthouse belonging to the Attorney General.

Sometimes I feel that the Wellington Testimonial is as near to Wellington College as I ever want to go.

> *OED* obelisk ... from οβελός ... spit, pointed pillar ...
> 1. a tapering shaft or column of stone, square or rectangular in section, and usually monolithic and finished with a pyramidal apex; a type of monument specially characteristic of ancient Egypt ... a needle...
> 2. a straight horizontal stroke ... or a mark used in ancient manuscripts to point out a spurious, corrupt, doubtful, or superfluous word or passage ... spit, obelisk, critical mark...
>
> to obelize ... to mark with a critical *obelos*: to condemn as spurious or corrupt in modern use applied to the mark † used in printing for marginal references, foot-notes, etc. a dagger
> *OED* sb 8. double obelisk – double dagger
> Learned commentators may *transfix* it with their obelisk of condemnation as spurious...

Maurice Craig, in his *Dublin*, describes: 'Robert Smirke's Colossus as a 205 foot obelisk ... placed on the only site in Dublin which could stand it ... the most massive structure of the city ... on the faces of its plinth are reliefs cast from the bronze of captured cannon...'

The Testimonial is an obelisk that needles republican hearts ... makes a critical (re)mark in Phoenix Park ... a spit of hubris in the eye of God ... but has no interior and none of Lord Nelson's swagger ... when you are near it you feel close to nothing ... the 'Iron Duke' was the 'hero of a hundred fights' in Tennyson's 'Ode on the Death of the Duke of Wellington'...

> Whose life was work, whose language rife
> With rugged maxims hewn from life...

And Maxim machine guns, under different names, were used by armies on both sides in the Great War to mow down brave young men ... like my father's brother, who led his platoon through a gap in a hedge on his first day rushing into battle at Ypres ... dying to become a photograph in a sacred book of 'Our Heroes' by his mother's bed.

Let 'Wellington College' be a sonnet of dedication to the art of poetry, thirty-nine years ago, as a result of which I am writing this poem today ... and let the 'Wellington Testimonial' express ironically the Duke's military command, his proud contempt for Ireland, his reserve and rigidity, and the force of his clear and cold laconic style ... which might have a bearing on my style in the sonnet ... I was sent to school in England, as he was, to train my tongue and to teach me manners ... his monument is exposed but reveals nothing ... no winding stair in its structure ... as tall as High Island of the saintly hermits off our west coast, but standing up in Dublin for the power of the Protestant Ascendancy to crush rebellion with merciless force.

 'We know what we are about ... no blockheads ... we ate the king's salt' ... a sonnet in the Duke's laconic tone of voice might send up the absurd illusion of immortality in verse or in stone ... playing with the obelisk's ambiguous situation today in Phoenix Park where the former Viceregal Lodge is occupied by the President of the Republic of Ireland ... the poem, unlike the monument for which it speaks, must, of course, have an inner life.

Overslept. Was awake before the alarm rang at 7.30, but didn't get up. Fell asleep for another hour. Time wasted. It was blowing a gale. Weather of my Connemara dream. Lazy habit of oversleeping in the west, because there was nothing that had to be done on time. Do not let either depressing weather or loneliness disrupt or dissipate the work. 'Wellington Testimonial' wasn't going so badly that I needed to give up.

 Like it or not, I carry the tone of the school in my voice and the style of the monument in my verse. Consider the situation of an Anglo-Irish obelisk, an immense landmark that has lost its purpose but kept its style. The poem should uphold the laconic style, the obvious point of common sense well made in the clearest words, without sacramental or ritualistic flavour. There was plain efficiency but no mystique surrounding the Iron Duke.

Why has the Testimonial not yet been blown up? Is Wellington preferred by republicans to Nelson? Surely not. Perhaps it *will* be blown up; except that nowadays the extreme republicans are using terror. Blowing up the obelisk would be a symbolic act inspiring mixed feelings, not terror. Think of the unfortunate driver of a school bus in County Tyrone last week, who was murdered on the bus in front of the children he was driving home.

The suffering caused by Wellington in the process of winning victories is something that the style of the testimonial – the laconic style – is trained not to feel or to reflect ... that is part of its strength, that it controls, ignores or suppresses or eliminates the kind of passions – especially feminine feelings – that would make the conduct of war between men more difficult to sustain. So Wellington's wife was kept at a distance where her emotions, her tears, would not confuse his mind. And I have kept the mother of my son at a distance for the same ignoble reason.

This is part of the Testimonial, the critical part. The laconic style is strong and clear, masculine and victorious, triumphal and heroic. Look where it leads us in the end ... on to a battlefield which it sees in terms of a game of chess, not of human lives destroyed in the pursuit of power. How many thousands of lost lives went into the erection of this monument to one man who survived a hundred battles ... honoured partly because people were amazed at his luck in not being killed in one of those hotly contested fights ... elected by God, as it were, to lead and always to win ... a super prize fighter with the pedigree of an aristocrat and the brains of a top civil servant.

Only at a distance is the monument beautiful. Close up it seems an emblem of brute force ... a colossal weight of circumstance ... cannon balls and pomposity ... power of the Union, the Crown, the Army ... to subdue a recalcitrant colony, as India had been subdued ... *that* aspect of the monument I loathe ... whores in the shrubbery after dark and civic guards stalking them ... guards of honour ... royal guardsmen in London pubs offering themselves as prostitutes ... their usual excuse, 'I'm not queer but saving up to get married'.

The poem might develop the ambiguity implied by the verb 'obelize' ... the critical remark must grow into self-criticism ... which is also a reflection on where and how I stand ... with an English voice in Ireland now ... in relation to the bronze reliefs, the embattled uncials, the colonial cenotaphic cult ... and all the people killed in the last world war for whom there can be no monument to match the evil of their extinction.

WELLINGTON TESTIMONIAL

Needling my native sky over Phoenix Park
I obelize the victory of wit
That let my polished Anglo-Irish mark
Be made by Smirke, as a colossal spit.

Properly dressed for an obsolete parade,
Devoid of mystery, no winding stair
Threading my unvermiculated head,
I've kept my feet, but lost my nosey flair.

My life was work: my work was taking life
To be a monument. The dead have won
Capital headlines. Look at Ireland rife
With maxims. Need you ask what good I've done?

My sole point in this evergreen oak aisle
Is to maintain a clean laconic style.

8 Dec 1982

Iggy McGovern

NORTHERN LIGHTS

C L Dallat, *The Year of Not Dancing* (Blackstaff Press, 2009), hb £12.99.
Michael Foley, *New and Selected Poems* (Blackstaff Press, 2011), hb £14.99.

Two welcome collections from the evergreen Blackstaff Press – the
Belfast house celebrates four decades of quality publishing this year. The
poets come from the north of Ireland but are both longtime settled in
London. Neither is as well-known in the south as they deserve to be.

The Year of Not Dancing is C L Dallat's second collection, some eleven
years after his début *Morning Star* (Lagan Press). That there is no rush
into print is evident in these carefully-wrought poems. The collection is
dedicated to the poet's mother, who died leaving a young family. There is
no doubting the eleven-year-old's pain of separation but emotion does
not overwhelm the writing. Instead the poems spread out to acknowledge
relations and neighbours in their spontaneous concern for the bereaved
children. In 'After Days in Blind-Drawn Rooms' the poet is comforted by
a neighbour who 'knew what you felt', recalling 'a brother she'd never
stopped thinking of since but / hadn't had much cause to mention, no
need until now.'

The setting for these childhood poems is the town of Ballycastle on
the North Antrim coast. By virtue of both its location and its religious
demographic, it has escaped the worst of The Troubles. Yet the fine
poem 'Difference' charts with humour and intelligence the residue of
religious apartheid that persists. Crawford Ballantyne is from the other
(Protestant) side and yet 'His people were more into / traditional dance-
tunes than ours.' He admonishes the poet *'Have some respect for your
culture –* / but no emphasis on the *your.'* But background will always out,
as in this, one of a pair of instances:

> And then at one of our funerals,
> he took second last lift of the coffin
> right to the gates and then neatly
> stepped aside. But it counted. That twice
> was more or less the extent of it.

The title poem of the collection has the teenaged poet 'in a last July
before the awkward initiations / of fifteen and lifts to far-afield jiving.'
When the music strikes up at the fairground, the not-yet-dancer sculls
out from the pier and looks back to see the 'dock and fairground small as

a snow-bubble town'. The image is locked in time by a snatch of the Frank
Ifield 1960s hit 'I Remember You', and there are similar references to pop-
ular music scattered throughout the collection; thus, The Teddy Bears rub
shoulders with Chuck Berry and Don McLean, all of them in my Top 100
but they are bound to send younger readers of these poems to Google.
Other localised cultural references may present a similar difficulty, although
this reviewer was (perversely) pleased that 'Dalton-Seimnitz series' in
'Getting Started' yielded an online blank – but that's computers for you!

Looking out from Ballycastle pier offers a view of Rathlin Island; in
Derek Mahon's eponymous poem its inhabitants are 'Custodians of a lone
light that repeats / One simple statement to the turbulent sea.' Possibly
this lighthouse (no longer manned) provides the inspiration for Dallat's
excellent poem 'Love on a Rock' (winner of the prestigious Strokestown
International Poetry Competition). The 'them' of the opening line – 'Who
could tell them now' – are the lighthouse children 'wiser in their
generations / than world-children', 'devouring a quarter's worth [of
comics] – / in a morning', 'hopscotching the one slab of cement / between
storm door and fairweather jetty'. It is packed with appropriate images
that both entertain and leave the reader unprepared for the last glorious
scene in which

> ...they'll have preset
> the Xerox's counter right up to the thousand,
> lid-up and nothing on the glass, eyelids
> numb on the margin of sleep as the phasings
> of light take them home to the beam-room again.

The last third or so of the collection takes us away from childhood and
The North, to far-off places, including the London of marriage and
children – 'do not watch the eclipse of the sun' is the advice offered to a
wife who can admit to 'being amazed that what's almost occluded / is
much more intense than what stares you fair in the face', but equally it
might apply to a father whose son and daughter have left home and he
hasn't 'once tuned the mandolin up since you sailed'. Alongside, and pre-
saging that departure, 'Bedsit' has the sixteen-year-old daughter enduring
the father's unspoken critique of her furnishings, that ends resignedly
with:

> OK, it's your room – who am I to quibble?
> I only knocked to ask, as it's May now
> And nights are lighter, whether you'll still
> Want your tartan-clad hot-water bottle filled?

Children and parents endure in their own amazing ways and this careful and caring collection is a fitting testament to that.

Michael Foley has an extensive publications list, including four novels and the four collections of poetry that supply the 'selected' in *New and Selected Poems*. Weighing in at 225 pages, this is a volume to last a whole year; indeed, the concept of an 'annual' is not inappropriate, given both the distinctive sectioning of the 'new' and the wide range of poetry sources, from the first millennium Chinese to the twentieth-century French poet and phenomenologist Francis Ponge. That combination in itself suggests that the reader unfamiliar with Foley's style might be advised to start towards the back of this marvellous book, perhaps even with the (after Ponge) 'Soap' that begins:

> Even manifold nature has nothing like soap.
> A cold bar can seem a stone, hard, self-contained,
> Withholding its essence in silent disdain
> And indifferent to water's unilateral kiss
> – But soap never desires the solipsism of stone.

And ends two-and-a-half pages later with:

> Put your sweet-smelling clean hands together for soap
> Which dissolves the seductive allure of the stone
> Whose apparent nobility it reveals as a sham.
> It is not strong but misanthropic, stingy and weak
> To justify the refusal to give by refusing to take.

Close observation, high vocabulary, acerbic humour, a lengthening line (they get longer) and a strong sense of the absurd are Foley's hallmarks. Nothing or no-one is sacred or safe from his wide-angled gaze. While Dallat's mother is a plaintive absence, Foley's is 'righteous and resolute' and she 'Even more savagely parts and combs flat / His hair' then 'marches him even / More forcefully to Church'. In this, the opening poem of the 'selected', the eponymous Poet Aged Seven sets out his stall, 'Oh anything loathsome and threatening', and climbs to 'the vertiginous attic crow's nest!'

That poem carries the rider 'after Rimbaud', and the list of French poets similarly acknowledged includes Laforgue, Apollinaire, de Dadelsen and Corbière (Foley has also published translations). 'Dream Home', after Tristan Corbière, begs comparison with Derek Mahon's 'Beyond the Pale' in its close-chiming opening lines but there are more than enough subsequent differences to allow for separate enjoyment. Although the comparison with Mahon goes beyond a shared interest in

French poetics, I imagine that Philip Larkin is the real mentor; the latter gets his due recognition in 'The king is half-dead, long live the king!', in which 'scary Philip's' witness is 'A mysterious simplicity and flatness / That carries such intensity and aptness.'

The toad work also gets the Foley treatment in this 'selection'. Again like Dallat, he has a background in computer science (surely he knows what a 'Dalton-Seimnitz series' is?). Thus, 'My briefcase' will 'go *anywhere* // Even to teach Information Systems to accountants / In the building where Pound gave his lectures / On troubadour poets'. The pedestrian job interview is transfigured in 'Heaven is waiting' in which 'Mr Wright... *of course*' is the one they were looking for. And it is, perhaps, the change of shift at the Du Pont chemical plant that prompts Foley's musings on his divided city of Derry / Londonderry in the splendid 'Talking to God on the new bridge over the Foyle'.

And, last but not least, there are the women; the mother again with her pithy colloquialisms in 'There's no call for the half of it'; the partner celebrated in 'The in-between song' – 'The lights low and half the band gone off for tea and a bun, / Once more we take the floor. The number is a smoochy one'; the first dancing partners' 'Great fleshy upper arms / with vaccination marks' ; and the unforgettable aunts advising the precocious scholar in 'A provincial adolescence':

> 'Don't be gettin' an eye for the girls whatever you do.
> Get all your degrees
> And *they'll* be runnin' after *you*.'
> They give him a briefcase for getting an 'A' and two 'B's.

Which brings us to the five-part 'new' section, which is titled 'Walking into Jerusalem'. Should the reader by now expect to meet the old joke about Christ tying his ass to a tree? The poems in the first part 'Solitary' range far and wide, just reading the titles is enough to turn your head – from 'Rosemary's baby' (that's Rosemary Tonks) to (my favourite) 'An old physicist faces the music'. I was less convinced by 'Pangur and I' but it's Biggles to the rescue (two books short of a century) in the next door 'The library in the desert'.

Two long poems and two sequences complete the section. 'The twisted grin' is a sexual romp through the court of Merrie England, while 'The parliament of the birds' retells the epic parable of the twelfth-century Sufi poet Farid ud-Din Attar, which tricks on the wordplay that Simurgh (God) is 'si' (thirty) and 'murgh' (birds) and, yes, I had to look that up. Even more knowledge lies in the 'Cold Mountain' sequence of poems in the voices of long-dead Chinese poets (I only knew of Li Po, courtesy of Mahon); they were civil servants, almost, to a man! – 'when you / Have to use the hierarchy, flatter it. Though as / Much down as up.' And, finally, 'The Book of Odes' brings us around the salons of Rome, or would do if the writers had not been banished. The penultimate word belongs to 'The retiring ode', the poet restored to the present day:

> Look to tomorrow's goat skull on a mountainside so today
> > Is warm flesh in the gardens of paradise.
> As I said to my Systems Design seminar: *The time box*
> > *Must be short to stop functional drift.*
> Youth that has everything is always the ingrate, and age
> > That has nothing the thanksgiver.
> In the taking away, the unlikely replenishing. Finitude
> > Is beatitude. The going is good.

In 2010 Michael Foley published *The Age of Absurdity: Why Modern Life Makes it Hard to Be Happy*. But this engaging and challenging *New and Selected Poems* will surely lighten the load.

Grace Wells

DÉBUT COLLECTIONS

Adam Wyeth, *Silent Music* (Salmon Poetry, 2011), €12.
Tom Duddy, *The Hiding Place* (Arlen House, 2011), €12.
Ailbhe Darcy, *Imaginary Menagerie* (Bloodaxe Books, 2011), £8.95.
Stephen Murray, *House of Bees* (Salmon Poetry, 2011), €9.60.
Noel Duffy, *In the Library of Lost Objects* (Ward Wood Publishing, 2011), £7.99.

Adam Wyeth's *Silent Music* opens auspiciously with 'Google Earth', a poem that a few years ago captured the zeitgeist of the early Internet age. It's an enigmatic piece that gilds the potentially mind-numbing activity of net-surfing with the deep magic of poetry. The poem begins hovering over Africa, with 'the world at our fingertips', and whizzes out from a white Mercedes parked in Harare, to a flash of 'our blue planet' before we zoom 'like gods' towards Ireland, following the Kinsale road and the Bandon river to 'our home framed in fields of barley', before 'the touch of a button' has us 'smack bang in Central London':

> the blank expressions of millions of roofs gazing
> squarely up at us, while we made our way down
> the avenue, as if we were trying to sneak up
> on ourselves; till there we were right outside the door:
> *the lunatic, the lover and the poet* – peeping through
> the computer screen like a window to our souls.

This is a seminal poem, but it's also something of a zenith. After a voyage from the exotic to the rural, from the urban to the soul, where can the poet go? The poems in *Silent Music* move from the sublime of 'Google Earth', not to the ridiculous, but often to positions of suave cool and downright negativity. Having trusted Wyeth as a safe guide, it's disconcerting to discover he isn't always going to take us to such luminous conclusions. 'The Long Run' is a similar voyage, moving through space and time, Wyeth directing the reader to run like we've never run before:

> run around the dark edge of Europe –
> run past the famine and diaspora,
> run through the uprising and the burning houses –
> run through The Republic and Troubled North.

We're to keep going 'past the ballot box of the Nice referendum / and the Lisbon Trick or Treaty':

go hell for leather to the Cliffs of Moher –
Now jump you daft eegit – *jump!*
In the long run we are all dead.

After such a *tour de force*, it's a disappointing finish, a dead-end that is echoed in 'Wannabe Poet', where Wyeth's narrator wants 'to wake in a war, / have my home ransacked, / and family shot'. A series of unfortunate events is wished for, and there's no redemption:

After I'm released,
coughing blood, I'll go to a tavern,
get stabbed –

then stagger downriver
scribble a quick note, and drown...
my body, unfound.

Silent Music voyages between extremes, we neither know where Wyeth will take us next, nor how he is going to bring us there. The collection is something of an experiment with form. At times Wyeth employs strict structures of rhyme or form. 'Waiting for the Miracle at Ballinspittle Grotto' is a haiku, 'Oxbow Lake' is a palindrome, 'Sycamore' is a concrete poem, '-Winged-Hope-' and 'Chimanimani Mountains, Zimbabwe' are peppered with Dickinsonian dashes. A spattering of poems must be read from the bottom of the page up. 'Telepathy' is a title on an empty page, and in 'Hell', every line ends with the word 'hell'. Wyeth is a one-man circus of dizzying acts. While there's an urbane, chameleon charm to all this, there's also the sense that *Silent Music* lacks a ringmaster with an identifiable voice: there's the temptation to ask, would the real Adam Wyeth please stand up?

Two questions hover over *Silent Music*. What kind of poet does Wyeth think he ought to be, and what does he consider poetry's purpose? The majority of the work is entertaining, witty and cosmopolitan; Wyeth is keeping his sails close to Billy Collins's wind. But this spirit of showmanship is at odds with the quieter, more refined voice that created 'Google Earth', 'Pinter's Pause', 'Robin' and the very lovely 'Blackout' – an unexpected piece about secret assignations between women during the London Blitz. Wyeth can take off his bravado and display a thoughtful vulnerability. 'Dad' and 'The Door' are particularly effective poems that reveal Wyeth as a writer of great stillness and great potential. A second collection will confirm the ground he wants, and really ought, to walk.

In complete contrast to Wyeth, Tom Duddy's *The Hiding Place*, has a consistent narrator. The voice is unwavering, mature, clear and precise in its intentions, lyrical in its thinking and feeling. Like the subject of his poem 'The Good Host', Duddy's collection 'is the one in whose humbling / and slow-darkening house / you cannot help but rest'.

The sounds of the collection are the clock's ticking, the rhythm of even and slow breath, the murmur of conversation, the overheard spoken in the vernacular. *The Hiding Place* has rural roots; the poems often concern themselves with the people, manners and customs of bygone, and fast disappearing, Ireland. 'Local History' begins:

> The men there, then, were most at peace
> when they clashed with the land itself,
> making light of the cut and thrust
> of the thistle in the cornsheaf.
>
> The women worked harder still, closer
> to the breath of animals, further
> removed with each passing year
> from their first dream of largesse.
>
> *Their farms have been swept clean*
> *into one far-reaching field, like*
> *a great clarifying idea inferred*
> *from a muddle of small dark thoughts.*

There's a grief throughout the collection for lost things, a sorrow over the houses fallen, the way of life gone, the dead. 'Nothing of that time or place remains. / Death and history have passed through them', Duddy writes in 'The Problem of Memory', but there's an acceptance too, a steady nerve, a lack of the hysteria that is present in some of the work of the other, younger writers reviewed here.

Duddy may be dealing in stock territory in terms of theme, but his craftsmanship and execution are entirely enviable. Duddy's poems are to be treasured. The work is beautifully paced, elegant; the poetry is solid and refined. For the student reader much can be gleaned from them about how poems ought to be made. Duddy has an enviable exactness of phrase. Each word and line has been carefully measured, and the stanzas carry their load without complaint or duress.

The harsh world rarely intrudes upon *The Hiding Place*. Duddy knows it exists, but he's more interested in moments of poise and poignancy. 'Brothers and Sisters', an excellent poem about the dark days of Irish schooling, shows a rare violence, but for the most part Duddy's poems collude to create a real hiding place: a refuge. In 'The Delivery Man', the gathered company unsurprisingly reach 'consensus on the lengthening /

of the days', but with the delivery man gone, the house 'closed in fast /
behind him and grew warm again, and airless / and secure. And
dreaming once more overcame us.' In city and country alike, Duddy
finds these sanctuaries, places where, as in 'Table for One', we can 'count
for something'. The real preserve of this book is shelter. The poems offer
us a place and a 'time to heal' (from 'Rest').

This is *The Hiding Place*'s gift and downfall, for Duddy's gentle hand
has a slightly soporific effect. When it all becomes too cosy, it's helpful to
turn back to 'Barns', an absolute cracker of a poem that takes us into
concrete, swallow-infested barns built by uncles in the 1930s where a
young Duddy...

> once drew out, tasselled with webs,
> the first real book I ever read, *The Thirsty Land* –
> cover of sunset-greens, a rifleman
> on the horizon turning in his saddle
>
> to view the great skull of a steer,
> the last chapters missing,
> leaving the main character, an Easterner,
> flailing in a burning barn, forever
>
> trying to free the screaming horses.

Like Wyeth, Ailbhe Darcy opens her collection with an arresting poem.
We read the title, 'Gone Fishing' and then the simple word, 'War.' It's a
perfect entry into Darcy's unique dominion.

> War. And one fierce girl
> will not take the bait.
> She swims off to stop it,
>
> leaves me dangling, thumb-sucking,
> plucking patterns from tea-leaves,
> scanning advice slips from bank machines,
> clutching at strings.

The poem continues on in an anarchic romp to end with Darcy's own
lack of certainty about whether to 'draw back / that girl-fish / or
tightrope out and join her / stitched fast to a bridge / over the Tigris.'
'Gone Fishing' works well, there's enough clarity for us to follow Darcy's
line of thought, enough linguistic lawlessness to know we've encountered
a rare mind. It is the balance of these two elements, or lack thereof, that
constitutes the drama of *Imaginary Menagerie*.

Darcy's poems are all kinetic energy. She rarely sits still, but dives from her lines, making mental leaps and forcing provocative diversions as if she's on a one-woman mission to oust complacency from poetry. Words fall down the page like so many pinballs in their machine, sounding off obstacles, striking bells, flashing lights, hitting a dizzying array of ideas and images. Added to which, Darcy is keen on unconventional vocabulary. The appearance of gems like 'bumbershoot', 'numen', 'quag', 'kickshaw', 'chain-shot', 'kerns', 'chawd-wine', 'bibelot', 'tchotchke' and 'fixfax', inhibit any easy apprehension of Darcy's intentions, and make it necessary to have internet access and/or a dictionary to hand.

Her strongest work is where her quirky, sometimes punk energy tunes itself to simple ideas. '*Aus der Mappe der Hundigkeit*' channels Darcy's urge for insurrection into the confines of a single argument to create a perfect political poem about Abu Ghraib. 'Panopticon' gently braids meditations on three tight themes: the terrible state of the world, Darcy's father, and Matthew 'who died last night at last of madness'. The result is a hauntingly lovely poem, an absolute keeper. 'The Art of Losing' balances ruminations on loss and on accumulation. 'Terminus' turns successfully on the idea of inviting an Arnold-Schwarzenegger-type Terminator to travel back to our times to sort them out. And 'Je me souviens' is a delightful road-movie of 'three Dun- / drum women at the peak of our powers' conquering Canada:

> We were circling thirty, sailed a rented
> vehicle stacked with hair straighteners, anti-
> perspirants, coconut M&M's and lip balm.
> We all had passable boyfriends.
>
> Adrift among accidents of translation
> the natives hardly noticed, let alone
> sanctioned or not-sanctioned our presence,
> but sure we'd invaded, without a harped ensign
>
> we'd taken the place.

Things get more complicated when Darcy shifts the weights on her scales. Whereas Duddy wants us to feel sheltered in the arms of poetry, Darcy's more comfortable with our having one of those tempestuous relationships where anything can happen next. The bulk of *Imaginary Menagerie* is a second tier of poems that come alive like rivers when read aloud but do not necessarily make entire sense, or even have discernable meanings. Still their race of words, their cacophony of sound, their shameless twisting of the breath and the lungs into new poses, combines to create a kind of shamanic experience.

Darcy changes tack so often it can be hard to know what her poems are about and if they have any specific centre of gravity. 'Market Square, Five Years After' is an engaging poem that begins with Darcy and her companion on a bench, eating baked potatoes, watching anti-war protestors. The second stanza ends: 'Is the world safer, then? / "No. It's not safer in Iraq" – Hans Blix.' In part two Darcy stands in a hotel shower 'shampooing my soul over and over / because I'm worth it'. She steps out to find the world gone quiet. She wonders,

> if something has happened outside while we
> were in here, if everyone has gone away to war
> or died. We will troop out together
> past the empty reception desk, the automatic
>
> doors parting to enable passage,
> the roads cleared of traffic. We can fill
> our rucksacks with food from abandoned
> stores, may have to move from hideout
>
> to hideout, or start our own farm. When I step out
> of the shower, you hold out your hand.
> I drop the towel to shake it.

We've gone on a stimulating voyage, but is the core of the poem a statement against war, a witty barb at consumerism, or a meditation on our ability to daydream while elsewhere the world burns? Perhaps all of the above. But why does she *shake* the hand? The word *take* would have brought the poem to a mood of intimacy; we would have known where to settle. As it is, we can't settle at all, the result is not so much a focused poem, but a provocative riff.

The collection advances and the mood of provocation casts a looming shadow, especially in poems like 'The Hotel' and 'Catacombs' where we are led to slightly baffling and insincere conclusions. In Darcy's most impenetrable work, staccato thought marries mundane material to generate rather dubious offspring. 'Dark Looker' opens:

> They rented the house by the quag for a fall.
> He was writing a history of landfill;
>
> she incubating, cooking kickshaw, the pair
> of them chain-shot on the porch.
>
> Locals warned them to beware the dark looker,
> and science, he answered, is the view from nowhere.

> She said nothing at that, only scored tight
> little crescents in the skin of her grapefruit,
>
> which oozed and was pellucid. Her far bits
> grew horny, her top end bees-wisped.

With perseverance we get a sense of what Darcy is saying, but we're left groping for the handrail of meaning that might give us the impetus to continue.

Reading *Imaginary Menagerie* with the intention of finding meaning makes for a very cerebral experience. To really get Darcy's work we need to go back repeatedly, re-reading her stanzas until they offer up their full theatre. Sometimes the poems simply don't reveal themselves. 'Telephone' (for Lady Gaga), is so full of twists and turns that it's possible to come away without any sense of personal engagement. The flamboyant riddles and disconnected shards Darcy lays before us make *Imaginary Menagerie* something of a Mensa gymnasium for the mind but collude to leave the collection a spectator sport for the emotions. 'Panopticon' is really the only poem where the spirit spontaneously soars. Nonetheless, a seam of terrific potential runs through the work and patient study gradually reveals the layers that Darcy has lain down in each poem.

Stephen Murray's *House of Bees* is one of the most interesting books Salmon have published in years. Poem titles foreshadow the book's territory: 'Memoirs of Woman's Aid', 'Tammy: Love in a Children's Home', 'Solvent Abuse', 'The Demon' and 'The Bottle in the Cupboard' all forewarn that the collection is something of an 'Adagio for Screams'.

Murray explores his material in a variety of different ways, some more successful than others. In 'House of Bees', 'A Love Letter for The Queen of Wasps' and 'The Drone That Got Away', Murray dives deep into a landscape of personal myth and bee metaphor that is quite difficult to follow. In 'The Looking Glass', characters from children's literature seem to be gratuitously imprisoned within a hellish adult world, where among other things, the Mad Hatter brings Alice 'dead flowers / then rapes her for hours'. A number of poems like 'An Irish Thing' and 'A Christmas Poem for A' help maintain a sense of menace, but rather struggle along without really pulling their weight. In 'Chronic Anxiety Jazz Solo', numbers one to four, Murray takes a cue straight from Dave Lordan's 'The Methods of the Enlightenment' and offers up a few of those state-of-the-art, rambling stream of conscious diatribes that some people think can be published under the title of poetry.

Yet we forgive Murray these trespasses because the book's true core is a gathering of unsurpassed autobiographical poems that sear the flesh. In 'Footprints', Murray reveals the bleak childhood crucible where he

and his sister became 'two tiny prints' that 'wandered off on their own /
seemed to fall to the ground then get back up / then fall to the ground
and get back up'. It's a sentiment echoed in 'Childhood' where:

> ...you're clumsy and you're of little use.
> You're just like your dad you deserve the abuse.
> Just like your parents deserve the excuse to the neighbour
> the preacher and the schoolteacher.
>
> *It really was nothing at all.*
> *I just bumped into wall*
> *after wall, after wall.*

There are other children in this world, children that appear in 'Memoirs
of Woman's Aid', children the 'divorce courts refused / invincible, brazen
and highly amused by our accents'. And children like Tammy, 'braless
and brainless and breathless and only thirteen', (from 'Tammy: Love in a
Children's Home'), who has no choice but to grow up to become
'Tammy on the Footbridge':

> Missing two teeth
> fishnets torn on turkey-thighs.
>
> Limping in high heels
> like Bambi on ice.
>
> Stitches in her lip
> a plaster on her swollen left eye.
>
> She tells me her second child
> has been taken from her
>
> placed in a House of Bees
> like the one we once shared.

Though Tammy is caught in the grip of addiction, she at least has fared
better than the 'you' addressed in 'Adagio for Screams' who is

> ...locked in some place where you are twelve again and your
> Mother stands dressed to the nines on the Dock Road
> pimping your ten-year-old brother, dressed as a girl
> to men made of whispers and spit.

Murray can't save these children and the adults they become, but his words, his plain speech, and his gift of tongues, catch them and offer a form of appalling redemption. And Murray knows that sometimes that's the only kind of redemption there is.

The book is held together by the excellent poem series 'Son of a Goat...' Parts 1-3, a distilled novel that moves through the different phases of Murray's life, so that by Part 2, toward the centre of the collection, the narrator has 'Pulled plastic bags over my own skull, filled them with puke and tears / Felt needles in my arms, found a treasure hunt of little brown bottles / with my very own name on them'. Towards the end of the book, in the fantastic 'Son of a Goat... Part 3', Murray meets a girl, takes the black bag off his head, and settles down, only to recreate his earlier nightmares. There's such wisdom and honesty here that it's impossible not to be entirely seduced. This is stunning poetry; it descends the dark fathoms only to pull us up airless, offering small flashes of surface grace before we're hauled back down for more.

Murray has a dramatist's discipline; he creates the maximum impact with the minimum words. Chiefly he employs a sparse, documentary style reminiscent of Raymond Carver and Charles Bukowski. Yet many of his poems are lit with a lyrical dynamism entirely Murray's own. *House of Bees* proves Stephan Murray a writer of extraordinary powers, who, with this material off his chest, could go on to do anything – though it will be hard for him to match the impact of what is achieved here.

In 'Rock Ammonite' Noel Duffy instructs us to close our eyes,

> and push one step further,
> past language and origins
> into the dark beginnings
> of it all.

In the Library of Lost Objects is underpinned by a strong awareness of the great age of our planet, of earth memory and the 'inner laws', so while Duffy is present in poems that relate to family, relationships and the intimate, part of him is ever alert to the 'furious energies of matter' (from 'A Stone'). Duffy perceives the profound in the natural world and translates it into lucid lines of poetry. In 'Fossil' he reads 'the braille of that ancient calamity / when the waters abandoned it', to see 'a kind of Christ etched in silicate'. In 'Baltic Amber' an ant caught in resin 'in the afternoon heat of the Palaeolithic' becomes an 'emblem and lifeline / of all that perishes, all that survives'.

In part, *In the Library of Lost Objects* is a natural history museum where the curator has found a way to let his exhibits, not only speak but also sing. In 'The Permanence of Stones' Duffy articulates a desire 'to go beyond the surface of things, to not just see the world and its objects but *be* the world and its objects, as sometimes he was in childhood.' He comes close. In 'Dragonflies' he watches the 'ghost geometries' of their flight and sees a demoiselle hover above the surface, 'a vector of pure thought'. Duffy is so tightly bound to the mysteries of bees and bee-keeping in 'The Beekeeper to His Assistant' that he could lend his name to a type of method writing in the same way that Lee Strasberg has given his to acting:

> You must understand from the beginning
> that the hive is a mind and one
> you will not comprehend. Behind
>
> the frantic to-ing and fro-ing of the bees
> order prevails: the honeycomb from nothing
> builds itself by geometry alone, cell by cell,
>
> the Queen its centre and circumference.
> Even the pollen-drunk dance of the messenger
> returned from gardens heavy with blossoms
>
> is a kind of mathematical waltz, calculating
> in each step the sun's slow orbit through
> the heavens.

Duffy steps from the natural world to the scientific. 'Apple' is a beautiful poem about Newton's moment, and the fruit's fall 'down to the ground / with a thud beside/the place he sits, to/start again the ancient act // of the naming of parts'. Einstein's love of science is traced back to the compass his father gave him for Christmas, 'a stopped clock, / the needle always pointing / north towards the spire' ('Einstein's Compass'). In 'The Moons' Duffy lyrically captures the moment Galileo discovered the moons of Jupiter in 1610, and 'The Mathematician at Midnight' is a tight but thoughtful rumination on the mysterious power of π (*pi*).

These faultless science and natural history poems are a strong presence, but they do not overpower, for the collection is perfectly balanced with poems of family and relationships, and poems about writing. 'The Book Collector' is dense with love for printing and writing and reading, and seems to hold the key to the success of the entire collection, for Duffy completely understands the elements that make good books. Moreover he understands the intimacy of reading. It's no accident that part three of this sequence, 'Inscription' ends with a hand-written note found in a second-hand book:

My Dearest James, In these pages we can be
together. Let us meet here in the white spaces

between one word's ending and another's beginning.
Love Kate. December, 1907.

Duffy is absolutely aware of the ways in which reader and poet meet and meld in the white spaces between words. He's entirely respectful of that relationship; he doesn't take us for granted, provoke or offend, or leave us lost and wandering aimlessly through his lines. Duffy understands poetry, it's his tradition; he obviously loves it and has a curatorial urge to see it thrive. He exhibits only the good stuff, the best work, there's no small talk, no gimmicks, nothing insincere, he just gets down to the heart of things and gives us poems that matter.

Duffy's relationship poems are nearly all about 'the slow unmaking of our happiness' – a lovely line taken from 'Your Photographs'. In his family poems he sketches people with the same considerate eye that animates stones. In 'Talking in Whispers', a favourite uncle is described as 'Wild in the way my mother was sober'. Duffy offers a number of powerful elegies to loved ones who seemed 'indestructible' but proved not to be. There is also a subtle rite of passage through the collection, which turns on Duffy's relationship with his father. The theme's development is book-ended by the poems 'Daisy-chain' and 'Swallows', but tenderly healed in the pivotal poem 'His Hands' where Duffy painstakingly recaptures – restores almost – his father's work as a sign-writer. The slow, meditative development of the poem leads Duffy to an awareness about his own craft, finding 'my father's touch in mine, / filling the unmarked page with words / / as night comes on'.

Repeatedly Duffy distills earthly experience into neat, elegant phrases that become touchstones which pass into personal vocabulary and enrich the ways we see and understand the world. In 'A Stone' he writes,

The furious energies of matter
are arrested here, made still for a moment
like a breath held under water.

In defining stone, he's defining his poetry. Duffy's 'naming of parts' impulse is richly captured in 'The Summer I Mapped the World', where a young Duffy takes to his bike to 'ordnance survey' the streets around his Dublin home. Ten potent stanzas later the job is done and Duffy reaches the new frontier of the Phoenix Park to see 'with shock, / the vast territory beyond'. He leaves the poem with a note of duality feeling 'something like defeat and freedom all at once'. It's a comfortable tension typical of Duffy, a writer who knows that *In the Library of Lost Objects*, we are found.

Gerard Smyth

SPEAKING FOR OTHERS

Brendan Kennelly, *The Essential Brendan Kennelly: Selected Poems* (Bloodaxe Books, 2011), £12.

> It was a gift that took me unawares
> And I accepted it

These lines from 'The Gift', the second poem in this selection and uttered early in the poet's journey, signal a clear declaration of his commitment. Since that ringing note of acceptance and throughout a long career, Brendan Kennelly, poet and teacher, has remained steadfast to his poetic pledge.

In their valuable and astute introduction, the editors (Terence Brown and Michael Longley) speak of Kennelly's 'predilection for publishing work thematically in selected editions with creative disregard' for chronology. Such was the case with his commodious collected poems, *Familiar Strangers*, which eschewed a timeline for a somewhat unorthodox approach, where poems often appeared side by side as rather odd bedfellows.

Here we have a chronological, as well as a representative and judiciously chosen, record of the poet's achievement that does, as the editors intend, give a sense of the 'shape and substance' of Kennelly poetic career – that career, and its significant contribution to the canon, deserves no less.

Kennelly is a poet of the wide embrace, as the Longley/Brown list demonstrates. Their 'essential' Kennelly covers a range of forms and content, from the concise and compact shorter lyrics – 'My Dark Fathers', 'Bread', 'A Kind of Trust', 'I See You Dancing, Father' and that magnificently affirmative favourite, 'Begin' – to extracts from the ground-breaking narrative sequences – *Cromwell* and *The Book of Judas* – that established him as one who took the side of the most demonised figures from history's hate-list.

It was Patrick Kavanagh who said that when a poet learns to speak for himself, he must then speak on behalf of others. Whether the older poet made this point directly to a young Kennelly is not known – but through-out his work the Kerry poet has always been conscious of this responsibility and fully attentive to it by allowing his poems to be the medium for a myriad of voices, a distinguishing characteristic of his work.

He allows those voices to address the reader directly through statement, plea, commentary, confession:

> I am that prince of liars, Xavier O'Grady,
> I am Tom Gorman, dead in the bog,
> I am Luke O'Shea, in Limerick prison…
> — 'AM'

Another familiar Kennelly device is the creation of a character or persona through whom the poet in fact vents his own thoughts – Moloney in the early poems, ozzie in *The Book of Judas*, Ace in *Poetry My Arse*.

From the outset he was a poet with a mission: his affinity with Kavanagh is obvious, he is the poet of 'proper praise' but he also knows when to unleash the scathing utterance, the Swiftian lash – against whatever: pomp, sanctimony, falsehood, the self-regarding ego, the vulnerability of society's victims. There is no posturing, his attacks are full-blooded – as Gerald Dawe has pointed out he assails the 'myth of Ireland with a vengeance'. There are certain Kennelly poems that surely afflict the comfortable, and comfort the afflicted.

Kennelly uses a crisp, pared-down language to great effect – one that is a model of clarity and always mellifluous. At times he is the poet of outrage – on other occasions the poet of tender empathy, a kind of Dostoyevsky-like empathy with the outsider, the maverick, the cipher, whoever might pass by unnoticed and unheeded.

He moves from the here-and-now to the mystical, a quality he shares with Kavanagh. One of his great strengths is his imagistic directness, there is too a deceptive ease to his Bardic style. Many of his poems exemplify Frost's contention that a poem 'begins in delight and ends in wisdom'.

> Whenever you walk smiling through a room
> And your flung golden hair is still wet
> Ready for September's homaged rays;
> I see what is, I wonder what's to come,
> I bless what you remember or forget
> And recognise the poverty of praise.
> — '"DEAR AUTUMN GIRL"'

There is something of the dissident in Kennelly; this is evident not only in his choice of subjects (Cromwell, Judas) but in the manner in which he appropriates and re-animates the language of the city street and rural village. Such places have provided him with the 'breathing spaces' that poetry requires. This Kerry poet may have forged his identity in Dublin, but the 'note of awe-struck wonder', referred to by his editors, was I sense something that came as part of his nurturing and initiations in the communal parish. It is also one of the most appealing attributes of this poet.

Of course, there are other Kennellys at work in these pages: a sharp laconic wit and a satiric touch that Swift would have admired have long been part of his arsenal – here is a poem worth quoting in full:

POINTS OF VIEW

A neighbour said de Valera was
As straight as Christ,
As spiritually strong.
The man in the next house said
'Twas a great pity
He wasn't crucified as young.

Along with this volume, another handsome Bloodaxe production, there are two bonuses: the CD of Kennelly's distinctive voice reading – or more likely reciting – these poems adds to the occasion, and gives us a real sense of their rhythmical elegance. The insightful and astute introductory commentary by Brown and Longley is valuable for both new and seasoned readers of Kennelly's work.

'A true poem is dreamed and danced as well as thought': the Australian poet Les Murray could have had Brendan Kennelly in mind when he made that statement. A Kennelly poem is both song and dance, its cadence and language carrying the reader to those places where the poet makes his own music and is in tune with himself.

Paul Perry

CHALK AND CHEESE

Billy Collins, *Horoscopes for the Dead* (Picador Poetry, 2011), £9.99.
August Kleinzahler, *Sleeping It Off in Rapid City: New and Selected Poems*
(Faber and Faber, 2011), £12.99.

Collins and Kleinzahler – they are no double act. American poets both.
Both born in the 1940s. Collins in New York. Kleinzahler in New Jersey.
Both have been laureates, albeit of two differing constituencies.
Kleinzahler of Fort Lee, Collins of the USA. That's where the similarities
end. Collins is the darling of popular poetry readers; his work is accessible,
pithy, breezy even. Kleinzahler, you will find at the opposite end of the
spectrum; his work is pugilistic, irreverent, iconoclastic and experimental.

If you have read any of Billy Collins's collections or even more than a
handful of his poems, you will not be surprised by what you find in
Horoscopes for the Dead, his ninth collection. But, like me, you may be
disappointed.

A great deal of the poems are first-person quirky dramas with a
recognisable but tired gesture towards metaphor. A favoured form is the
tercet. There's a safeness to the method, a feeling that Collins is in his
comfort zone, even when an Irish connection is pressed home in several
poems. 'The Snag' opens with a typical yawning address:

> The only time I found myself at all interested
> in the concept of a time machine
> was when I first heard that baldness in a man
> was traceable to his maternal grandfather.

The cartoonish imagination of Collins pictures the poet 'stepping into
the odd craft / with a vial of poison tucked into a pocket'. Then he sets
the 'coordinates / for late 19th century County Waterford', where he
would 'enjoy several whiskeys and some talk / about the hard times...'

Time and time again, I felt a falling inconsequence to the poems in
Horoscopes for the Dead. They are too clever and cutesy for their own good.
Self-proclaimed 'secretary of the interior', Collins's writing is lucid, at
times child-like, but it is also full of weary adult platitudes. In 'Memento
Mori', Collins is off to Cork after looking in 'a magazine' and seeing the
Church of St Anne. Mortality is *the* theme of the collection and in the
same poem we read that there are 'So many reminders of my mortality /
here, there, and elsewhere'. There's a home-grown wisdom and a kind of
'trust me' inflection within the work which contains a stultifying lack of

tonal variation; the lyrics come at you with the monotonous resignation and existential sigh of 'Oh well'.

There's also a saturation of first-person mini-dramas. Mostly the poet forges a first-person persona which suggests implicitly that the 'I' in the poems is the poet himself. This self-reflexivity is an over-bearing strategy. Too often, Collins addresses the reader in an all too 'knowing' manner. In 'Gold', for example, Collins writes 'the last thing I want to do / is risk losing your confidence / by appearing to lay it on too thick' after comparing the sun in Florida to 'the fire / that Aphrodite lit in the human eye'. The meta-note becomes cloying the more we hear it, for example when 'the subtropical sun' warms 'this page' in 'Thank-You Notes', or in the arch 'Poetry Workshop Held in a Former Cigar Factory in Key West', where Collins compliments himself on never drawing an analogy between 'cigar-making and poetry'. His self-satisfaction and *voilà* magicianship takes us to the shrug-inducing final stanza:

> Not once did I imply that tightly rolling an intuition
> into a perfectly shaped, handmade thing
> might encourage a reader to remove the brightly colored
> encircling band and slip it over her finger
> and take the poet as her spouse in a sudden puff of smoke.
> No, I kept all of that to myself, until now.

Earlier books may have achieved a fresh and quirky note, but the work in *Horoscopes for the Dead* does not look like it has evolved from there. When he strives for poignancy, Collins often reverts to formula and falls flat. In 'The Straightener', he presents himself as a person with a mild compulsive disorder, 'Today for example, I will devote my time / to lining up my shoes in the closet …' At other times he is a *flâneur* in Florida:

> Who needs Europe? I muttered into my scarf
> as a boy flew by on a skateboard
> and I fell into a reverie on the folly of youth
> and the tender, distressing estrangement of my life.

The poems have a Garrison Keillor ring about them; the reassuring tones of experience and *faux*-wisdom. But for me, the work doesn't make the reader care enough. What's at stake in these poems?, I asked myself reading. The ironic and clever title left me thinking that the dead need horoscopes as much as the living. That's to say …

The surprise, risk, and urgency lacking in Collins can all thankfully be found in August Kleinzahler's protean *Sleeping It Off in Rapid City*, his New and Selected Poems. Within this substantial offering, made up of poems from *Red Sauce, Whiskey and Snow, Green Sees Things in Waves, Live from the Hong King Nile Club*, and *The Strange Hours Travelers Keep*, there is an exciting bravado, an unpredictable and visceral intelligence and energy at work.

Kleinzahler has written and talked of the strong influence and inspiration Basil Bunting and *Briggflatts* in particular has made on him. Certainly, there is a modernist bent to his work, but there's also a gusto to his sometimes manic imagination. Take for example, the opening and title poem 'Sleeping It Off in Rapid City', a six-page rhapsody which begins:

> On a 700 foot thick shelf of Cretaceous pink sandstone
> *Nel mezzo ...*
> Sixth floor, turn right at the elevator
> "The hotel of the century"
> *Elegant dining, dancing, solarium*
> Around the block from the Black Hills School of Beauty

Kleinzahler's poems are much more a poetry of becoming or process rather than Collins's poetry of being and product. Like Hopkins, Kleinzahler follows the movements of his mind, wherever they take him, and to some weird and wonderful places they do take him. In this one opening poem the reader will encounter Dante, a closed dinosaur shop, the lambs of Christ, Lakota sandstone, the 'ghosts of 98 foot long Titans and Minutemen', Crazy Horse, sacred bison, Kevin Costner, Babe Ruth and Calvin Coolidge, who all appear in a heady rambunctious ode to America.

Kleinzahler's work is nothing like Emily Dickinson, but like her he tells all the truth, but tells it slant. The side-ways glance often ricochets from demotic registers to more lofty accents. In 'Shoot The Freak', popular cultural references to SpongeBob, Spookerama and Luna Park sit next to Miles Davis's *Sorcerer*, The White House and Lady Di:

> ("a great person, just a fabulous person, a real human being")
> I mean how good is this, really, I mean really, seriously, how good is this

Kleinzahler's restless intelligence creates a host of voices, a polyphony of textures from the mean streets of New Jersey or San Francisco to the sequential consideration of the history of Western Music. In 'Secondary Sexual Characteristics', there's an almost Joycean relish in the senses:

> *Relish of wild duck cooked with olives*
>
> *The slight scent of prussic acid*
>
> *A faint whiff of overripe peaches*

His Poundian dictum could be, in his own words, '*Études endocrines*'. There's a scientific knowledge on display here, an encyclopaedic range of reference, and a capacious humour which is often enough tinged with the scatological. He ends the same poem with:

> Eyes like slits
> Poor Pip
> Drool at his lips
> Caught up in a proper fit
> A 9-cycloheptadecenone-addled marionette
> Mewing
> > – *Kill me, fuck me, write me bad checks*

His wild humour is sometimes tempered by a vocational resilience. In 'Goddess', a Gravesian muse-poem, he writes:

> I know better than to implore,
> complain, or like some schoolchild, wish.
> Unvisited I do not live, I endure.

Born and brought up in New Jersey, Kleinzahler's voices can register an elastic range. In 'Meat', he brings the industrial hinterland of his hometown into a cinematic focus:

> They arrive, numberless
> Hauling tons of dead lamb
> Bone and flesh and offal
> Miles to the ports and channels
> Of the city's shimmering membrane
> A giant breathing cell
> Exhaling its waste
> From the stacks by the river
> And feeding through the night

Feeding through the night, as his imagination does, a nocturnal kaleidoscope where 'Loneliness – huge, suddenly menacing' creates a poetics of disenchantment and dislocation, and yet even with the hurly-burly of his longer poems you will also find poems, when you least expect it, of simplicity and tenderness. In 'Late Indian Summer':

> Nights already belong to winter.
> You know by that tuning fork in its jacket
> of bone
> broadcasting to the body's far ports.

Days like this so late in the year
inflame desire, perturb
the ground of dreams, and roust us from sleep,
exhausted and stunned.

And 'Before Dawn on Bluff Road', where the 'chemical ghost of old factories' brings Kleinzahler to:

> ...my childhood room
> with its fevers and dreams.
> My old parents asleep,
> only a few yards across the hall,
> door open – lest I cry?
> I remember
> almost nothing of my life.

Kleinzahler can be the cynic, the sardonic, the hustling fevered, impassioned voice in American poetry – and as if responding to the credulous and naïve lyrics of Collins in 'Grave' where the speaker invents...

> the business
> of the one hundred Chinese silences –
> the Silence of the Night Boat,
>
> and the Silence of the Lotus,
> cousin to the Silence of the Temple Bell
> only deeper and softer, like petals, at its farthest edges.

...Kleinzahler in 'The Bus Barn at Night' writes that:

> *Motion is not a condition*
> *but a desire*
> *to be outside of one's Self*
> *and all desire must be swept away*
>
> so saith fatso Gautama
> bus-like
> under the shade of some shrub
> in the Deer Park

His *New and Selected Poems* is rich and fiery, unpredictable in its trajectory, brimming with invective and wit, aggressive even in its devil-may-care attitude and always compelling.

Thomas Dillon Redshaw

THE LIVING VOICE

The Penguin Book of Irish Poetry, edited by Patrick Crotty (Penguin Classics, 2010), hb £40.
An Anthology of Modern Irish Poetry, edited by Wes Davis (Harvard University Press, 2010), hb $35.

Published almost back-to-back, Patrick Crotty's and Wes Davis's generous and substantial anthologies of Irish poetry, the first a Penguin Classic and the latter from Harvard, will loom large on library shelves and in library catalogues worldwide. Sturdy, weighty, handy, each is an island of real print – an Inis Mhicéal – buffeted by tides of virtual publication. Both propose a canon of authors and works deriving from the several revivals of writing in Ireland that distinguish the astonishing and fraught culture of twentieth-century Ireland – from the Gaelic Revival and the Literary Revival through the Rising and Troubles, and the Emergency, from the second revival of the 1960s and 1970s through the 'Troubles' in the North. Since the arrival of the Normans, such revivals have characterised the periodicity of the island's oral and written literary culture – a culture tending always to gather itself when under threat. And, for Crotty's anthology, Penguin's graphic designers have underscored these ambitions with their jacket design, whose deep purple rose alludes tellingly both to 'An Róisín Dubh' and to Yeats's beginnings in Blake, by way of the two graven worms crawling the green leaves.

While Davis alludes to such prior anthologies as Paul Muldoon's eccentric *Faber Book of Contemporary Irish Poetry* (1986), as well as Crotty's own Blackstaff anthology of 1995, *Modern Irish Poetry*, his selection of Irish poets and poems from Padraic Colum (1881–1972) through to Sinéad Morrissey (b. 1972) comes across as less formed by prior anthologies than Crotty's selection of lines and verses dating from the ninth century, in part because Davis's interest lies in the '*modern*, in the sense of recent, rather than *modernist*' (Davis xxiii). That is to say that Davis's focus tends toward what poems and poets are presently being published by Peter Fallon's Gallery Press (the inheritor of much of the Dolmen list):

> Peter Fallon has had a hand in the publishing of nearly every poet in
> this collection. As the founder of the Gallery Press, Fallon has
> given a public outlet to rising Irish writers who benefit from the
> authority the press earned early on... (Davis 617)

In that well-deserved commendation of Fallon's enterprise, Davis recognises the facts of Ireland's recent literary history. Consequently, Davis's attentions fall less on Bloodaxe and Carcanet (the inheritor of the Oxford list), much less on Dedalus – John Ennis and Enda Wyley being the only Dedalus poets in his selection – and some on Raven Arts and Lagan, but not at all on Salmon. In contrast, Crotty's reach stretches way back into the remains of the ninth century, back as far as John Montague reached in 1974 with his *Faber Book of Irish Verse*. Like Montague's prior reach, Crotty's has motives both Modernist and Romantic that find fine expression in the care Crotty takes with poems and songs composed in Irish.

Reviewers in Dublin and London have stressed the presence of Irish-language poets in both anthologies – particularly the coming into English of Seán Ó Ríordáin – but the Penguin Book better registers the enduring presence of Gaelic composition, which Gerald Mangan has ably parsed in the *TLS* (27 May 2011). Of particular interest here is Crotty's presentation of Brian Merriman's *The Midnight Court* – the touchstone of vernacular Gaelic poetry – in tandem with Oliver Goldsmith's *The Deserted Village*, and from the hands of four translators: Carson, Heaney, Kinsella, and Frank O'Connor. Behind Crotty's marshalling of the Gaelic inheritance in his Penguin Book lie anthologies that have been a godsend to late twentieth-century readers, teachers, and writers: Osborn Bergin's *Irish Bardic Poetry* (1970), Thomas Kinsella's *An Duanaire* (1981), Dermot Bolger's *The Bright Wave / An Tonn Gheal* (1986), and *An Crann Faoi Bhláth / The Flowering Tree* (1991). Because of his narrower temporal scope, Davis gives us Máirtín Ó Direáin, Nuala Ní Dhomhnaill, and Cathal Ó Searcaigh, but no translations of Michael Hartnett or Pearse Hutchinson (whose English verse makes the cut), and nothing from, say, Cáitlín Maude or Liam Ó Muirthile, let alone from Eoghan Ó Tuairsc, whose *Aifreann na Marbh* (1964) stands with Kavanagh's *The Great Hunger* (1942) as one of the more remarkable achievements of Irish poetry at mid-century.

Of course, readers in Ireland (and many outside it) will begin to name the names of those in the *salon des refusés* – and particularly so in the case of Davis's anthology, which gives 900 odd pages to fifty-two poets – leaving out the late Patrick Galvin and John F Deane, for instance. It is a jolt to find so much from Richard Murphy's *The Battle of Aughrim* (1968) and less from John Montague's *The Rough Field* (1972). It is refreshing to have C Day Lewis along with Louis MacNeice, Michael Hartnett along with Paul Durcan, John Ennis with Dennis O'Driscoll. Readers will find titles they know and expect, among them Kavanagh's 'Epic' or Boland's 'The Achill Woman'. Other of Davis's choices prove to be keys to the poet's world, like Thomas McCarthy's 'The Non-Aligned Storyteller' or Paula Meehan's 'Take a breath. Hold it. Let it go'.

In contrast, Crotty's portrayal of the same decades of literary history (1922–2009) takes almost 300 pages and presents some fifty-five poets in a richer, curiosity-inciting critical design. Readers will note a signal feature of that design when they notice that some poets appear twice – Yeats, Clarke, Kinsella, Montague, and Murphy – thus making plain Crotty's emphases. Of course, Crotty offers Ó Direáin and Ó Ríordáin, Boland and Ní Chuilleanáin, but he offers also F R Higgins, Padraic Fallon, Máire Mhac an Tsaoi, as well as such younger contemporaries as Kerry Hardie and Greg Delanty. But, again, nothing from Galvin. The Irish presses – not only Gallery, but also Raven Arts and Sáirséal agus Dill – come well represented and augmented by Crotty's attention to the poets printed in Britain, not only by Faber and Carcanet, but also Cape, and Chatto and Windus. Crotty's selections register the fact that Irish poetry has gained in Britain a regular critical 'reviewership', which it had not quite earned back when Montague compiled his Faber anthology in 1974.

Readers who plunge unwarily into the midst of these pages will find that Crotty has overlaid or 'orchestrated' his chronological arrangement with groupings by genre, both expected –'Epigrams' – and unexpected subject genres like 'Heroes'; with broadly conceived rubrics of cultural period, like 'Civilizations' or, more familiarly, 'Revival'. Historically speaking, Crotty's awareness that, especially after the coming of the Normans, poets and their poems not only inhabited at least two linguistic realms and audiences, they also found themselves at the threshold – sometimes starving, sometimes rewarded – between two cultural periods. So it is that major figures can appear twice. Yeats strides through the 'Revival' (1881–1921) and into 'The Sea of Disappointment: 1922–1970', and Clarke as well. With the title 'Transformations',' Crotty invites us to characterise more exactly the third and fourth periods of Irish poetry, dating from 1971 through to the Good Friday Accords of 1998 and into the rise and fall of the Celtic Tiger. What poets might stand on that Millennial threshold? Kinsella, Boland, and certainly Heaney.

Like Montague's introduction to his *Faber Book* – titled 'In the Irish Grain' – with a little editing Crotty's introduction will find its separate way into future practical criticism – and into handy collections of criticism and commentary like Theo Dorgan's *Irish Poetry since Kavanagh* (1996) or *Flowing Still* (2009). While Crotty's introduction is not a Thomas Davis lecture, his paragraphs and sentences carry the hallmarks of the thoughtful, speaking voice proposing with ease and confidence an historical vision and a novel arrangement of Ireland's more than bilingual poetic traditions. Crotty offers a complete, judicious, and above all helpful argument that has been fruitfully shaped by prior scholarship ranging from the cumbersome *Field Day Anthology* (1991) to Andrew Carpenter's *Verse in English from Eighteenth-Century Ireland* (1998). For a sympathetic, synoptic account of Crotty's critical sensibility, one cannot do better than Barra Ó Seaghdha's extensive *Dublin Review of Books* essay (**www.drb.ie**, Winter 2010-11), which justly notes Crotty's thematic emphases. And here is another:

> The dividing line between 'poem' and 'song' is similarly permeable. [...]
> [P]oems are intended for recitation or private reading, while songs are
> primarily meant to be sung. (Crotty lxii)

Crotty's farewell observation that the words of Robert Burns's 'Laddie lie near me' remain 'inert without the melody' and that 'the power of the song is revealed only in performance' reveals his critical stance, one so old-fashioned as to seem postmodern. The poems Crotty has selected are not only texts, not just mental constructs, but unmistakable instances of Irish voices at play and persuasion, at devotion and passion, at celebration and mourning. Crotty could hardly make his emphasis plainer: 'I have been guided by my sense of the verbal life of the material...' (Crotty lxxxvi). Hardly a poem in these pages inhabits the mind or heart without first commanding the tongue, and so it is the living voice – *an glór beo* – speaking in monologue or singing out in hymn or ballad – that Crotty has listened for, heard, and collected for us. And this is why the Hiberno-English of the eighteenth century – macaronic or parodic, quarrelsome or sentimental – interests Crotty as much as the long lines of nationalist and newspaper balladry, or the few remains of Middle English of the heartlands of Norman Ireland, or the petitions and prayers of monastic Ireland.

Like Crotty's *Penguin Book*, Davis's *Modern Irish Poetry* goes without extensive academic apparatus – textual notes, glosses, clues to allusions – all those Norton Anthology 'helps' that can reward and sometimes can mislead readers. Davis makes up for this by offering an introduction and authors' notes that seem 'undersourced' in that they take only partial account of the tide of critical writing on such poets as Kinsella and Boland, Carson and Ní Dhomhnaill, published in Ireland, Britain, and North America. The contours of Davis's portrayal of Irish poetry since Yeats (or Joyce, or Kavanagh) owe much to such prior accounts as those by Dillon Johnston (1986) or Neil Corcoran (1997). Arriving at the 'remarkable accomplishment of the Belfast poets', Davis suspends his critical story in favour of fifty-three sometimes dutiful author's notes.

Both Davis's introduction and his notes can offer oddly out-of-focus observations. For example, by way of arguing (again) the chestnut that John Montague's repute lies in 'stylization', Davis says '...in the North, John Montague was writing about the texture of daily life in rural Tyrone', but in the 1950s and 1960s Montague was working, teaching, and writing in Dublin and Paris (and the United States), publishing in Dublin with Dolmen and in London with MacGibbon and Kee. The publication record is plain. Or, in respect to Kinsella, that quintessential Dolmen poet, Davis's author's note concludes that 'Peppercanister has published Kinsella's occasional verse ever since' *Butcher's Dozen* in 1972. Indeed, 'occasional verse' seems hardly the term for such Peppercanister sequences as *A Technical Supplement* (1976) or *The Pen Shop* (1997).

These two anthologies finish off a crescendo of Millenial canon-building that had its start and inciting motive in *The Field Day Anthology* (1991). In the decades since, editorial industry and scholarly invention have paraded to the big world Ireland's literary accomplishment and cultural confidence dating from the 1890s. Yet, at this very present moment when the world of the word increasingly declines physical incarnation on the bound page, the impulse to anthologise so monumentally may also betoken a certain anxiety in Irish literary sensibilities – the same sort of anxiety about the immediate (English) future that motivated the Gaelic literati of the seventeenth century – Geoffrey Keating, the Four Masters – to gather the lore of the Gaelic Order into books and notebooks, chronicles and poem-books. Davis's and Crotty's anthologies will reside in libraries the world around. If libraries increasingly become digitised 'places for people' and not for books – the Manchester Central Library lately disposed of 300,000 volumes from its main collection – then what sorts of anthologies may serve the practising Irish poet at home or abroad?

Given time and patience, Irish poets writing now will learn much from *The Penguin Book of Irish Poetry*. Yet, the anthologies that have wound up mattering most to the practising poet are the odd ones that do not travel well. Sometimes these are exotic like Donald J Carroll's *New Poets of Ireland* (1963). Sometimes these are regional, like *The Inherited Boundaries* (1986) or *Map-Maker's Colours* (1988) or *Jumping Off Shadows* (1995). And sometimes the most invigorating turn out to be clique or coterie selections, posed often as generational manifestoes and disguised as broadsheets, a genre that yet survives in Ireland, or the 'little magazine'. And because, over the decades, Crotty has taken these venues for poetry into his ken, many of his well-poised selections from the Irish traditions will hearten the writer at his or her table near a rainy window. Pencil in hand or keyboard at the ready, the practising poet may be emboldened by such of Crotty's observations as this: 'Purely in terms of poetry, the decades since 1970 are more deserving of the "renaissance" label than the literary movement led by Yeats nearly a century earlier…" (Crotty lxxxv).

Proinsias Ó Drisceoil

CALVIN AND CATULLUS

Iain Crichton Smith, edited by Matthew McGuire, *New Collected Poems*
(Carcanet, 2011) £18.95.
The Irish Catullus or One Gentleman of Verona, edited by Ronan Sheehan,
(A and A Farmar, 2010), €20.

Iain Crichton Smith's *New Collected Poems* is not the collected poems it
claims to be. Indeed given that it is already 546 pages long, it could hardly
encompass omitted material without becoming a two-volume set. What
is more significant than the omitted poems in English however is the fact
that Smith's poetry in Scottish Gaelic appears only in translations which
were originally included in various English-language collections. No
doubt their inclusion would require a linguistic competence which may
not be among the editor's attainments.

Not that any of this would have upset Smith himself. Born in Glasgow
in 1928, he grew up in Bayble on the Isle of Lewis, where he spoke Gaelic
to his poor, widowed mother as their home language. Nonetheless his
strained and troubled relationship with Gaelic was such that it is surprising
that he wrote anything at all in the language, let alone an extensive and
distinguished output of poems, short stories and novels. He saw Lewis as
a place where any trace of culture had been eroded by Calvinism and saw
his discovery of the literature and expressive powers of English as offering
access to a world of self-understanding and intellectual nourishment that
Lewis consciously proscribed. While advocates of Gaelic saw the ferocity
with which English was promoted as the sole language of the schools as
a form of cultural tyranny, Smith saw his education at all stages, and at
Aberdeen University in particular, as a journey into enlightenment, and
his ever-extending knowledge of English literature – and of the wider
arts – allowed his poetry to benefit from a wide range of influences.

As an atheist, art had taken the place of religion but a Calvinist guilt
dogged belief in his own creative work: 'for the islander to be influenced
by T S Eliot or William Carlos Williams instead of Duncan Ban Macintyre
is almost to be a traitor', as he wrote in his critical volume *Towards the
Human*. Indeed one might wonder if Smith's frankly-acknowledged bouts
of mental illness were not in part a product of a belief that art was a
form of vanity, the Calvinist sin of sins.

Perhaps it was their shared history of mental illness that made the
poetry of Robert Lowell such an influence on Smith's work, perhaps too
much so in particular instances, such as in the Lewis section of his long
poem 'A Life' (1986) where Lowell's 'Waking in the Blue',

> I grin at Stanley, now sunk in his sixties,
> once a Harvard all-American fullback...

becomes localised to a...

> Once famous footballer. He's alcoholic now.
> He'll speak to no one, crying through bare rooms...

Lowell, Eliot and, above all, Auden helped Smith to develop a style in which intense emotion could be granted enhanced emphasis through control over form. However this anxiety for influence can sometimes give an unresolved quality to his work and his style was never entirely settled or defined.

Smith regarded his English poem, 'Deer on the High Hills' as his best, and its inscrutability and mystery, as well as its Dantean form, give substance to the many claims which have been made for it:

> Yesterday three deer stood at the roadside.
> It was icy January and there they were
> Like debutantes on a smooth ballroom floor.

However the more localised literature of Scottish Gaelic gives a specificity and bareness, an economy and an unfinished starkness to his poems in that language that makes it among his pre-eminent achievements. 'Tha thu air Aigeann M'Intinn' / 'You Are at the Bottom of my Mind' must be one of his best poems. In it he explores the ineffable, an unreachable elusiveness which does not lend itself to easy summary:

> Without my knowing it you are at the bottom of my mind, like one
> who visits the bottom of the sea with his helmet and his two great eyes:
> and I do not know properly your expression or your manner after five
> years of the showers of time pouring between you and me...

This and other Gaelic poems are often not helped by rather indifferent authorial translations, emphasising again the poet's tortured attitude towards his mother tongue, with both mother and tongue being sites of neurosis. The index has eight poems entitled 'Old Woman' as well as three entitled 'Old Lady' and a variety of similar titles. The persistence of this theme reveals the poet's unresolved relationship with his mother and with a dour Calvinist practicality which denied all beauty and culture:

> Your set mouth
> forgives no one, not even God's justice
> perpetually drowning law with grace.
> – 'OLD WOMAN'

Paradoxically, given the character of the translations of his own work, translations from Gaelic are among Smith's greatest achievements. The international reputation of Sorley Maclean derives in large measure from Smith's 1971 translations of Maclean's *Poems to Eimhir*, and his translations of eighteenth-century long poems such as Duncan Ban Macintyre's 'Ben Dorain' and Alexander Macdonald's 'The Birlinn' are outstanding in their engaged transmission of the spirit of the originals.

Smith's poetry struggles to embrace what *is* rather than what might be. For him 'Writing / is easier than experience' but it is of experience that he seeks to write.

Ronan Sheehan has marshalled whole divisions of the poetic standing army to proffer versions of the Latin poems of Gaius Valerius Catullus (c. 84 BC – c. 54 BC) in English and Irish. Each poem is offered in parallel versions – across the broad pages of landscape format – in Irish, the Latin original and in English. Indeed the inclusiveness of the project is such that the Gaelic versions are, in certain instances, offered not in Irish but in Scottish Gaelic and, on one occasion, in Manx. The book originated as a response by Sheehan and the board of Poetry Ireland to the decision by Queen's University Belfast to close its classics department. Ironically, the book itself is an illustration of why interest in the classics has reached this sad stage: one gains the impression that actual translations – versions deriving directly from the Latin originals – constitute a minority of the poems in the book. Where versions are based on the original Latin they are generally the work of those of us old enough to have learned Latin when it was in effect a compulsory subject in many secondary schools.

Quite a number of contributors abandon any attempt at translation in favour of what aim to be witty responses, alluding to Bertie Ahern, tribunals of enquiry and the likes. 'CXII', a sixteen-word poem becomes twenty-eight words in Micheál Ó Ruairc's Irish and a full page in Mia Gallagher's English. Among those clearly working from the original Latin, Deirdre Brennan is truly outstanding and her versions in Irish are significant poems in their own right:

> Dianae sumus in fide
> puellae et pueri integri;
> Dianam pueri integri
> puellaeque canamus.

> Muidne tairisigh Diana,
> cailíní óga is buachaillí íonghlanta,
> canaimis caintic Diana,
> buachaillí is cailíní íonghlanta.

Like Manx, Latin has never altogether died. Hopefully, neither language ever will.

Liam Carson

SILENT CITIES

Simon Ó Faoláin, *As Gaineamh* (Coiscéim, 2011), €7.50.
Caitríona Ní Chléirchín, *Crithloinnir* (Coiscéim, 2010), €7.50.

Poet and archaeologist Simon Ó Faoláin sees the act of writing poetry as
akin to that of the archaeologist's task of imagining or re-creating a lost
or forgotten world. His latest collection *As Gaineamh* uses the language of
digging and probing, scrutinising and examining, to investigate both the
making of an individual and the world in which he or she lives. It's heady,
ambitious stuff. Ó Faoláin's Irish is immersed in the speech of Corca
Dhuibhne, and many of his poems are driven by strong rhythms and
rhymes. These are well-honed metrical poems with echoes of early Irish.

Ó Faoláin's confident poems are replete with images from modern
science. These are put to sometimes stunning effect, as in 'Sa Tigh
Altranais, Gleann na Deargaile, Cill Mhantáin'. With his grandmother in
a nursing home he joins her on an imaginative voyage to her childhood,
and blurs the distinction between the generations. He sees himself
travelling to the 'pre-history' of an individual, evokes atoms splitting, DNA
helixes, and finally the dust that we all are:

> Níl ann anois ach dhá neach,
> Siar tré rannta chlós na scoile
> Go réamhstair an duine aonair.
>
> Scoiltear an t-adamh, léitear héilics dúbailte go grinn,
> Ach choíche ní ríomhfar dúinn an folús i lár baill.

The title poem 'As Gaineamh' has as its epigraph a quote from Beckett
('*Je suis ce cours de sable qui glisse entre le galet et la dune...*'), and has three
sections. He describes an evening beachcombing, coming across a plaster
doll wrapped in seaweed, then shifts to an archaeological dig that
uncovers a Viking keel that shatters when moved, before moving into a
final vision of the birth and death of the universe.

'Do dhuine fén mbráca' addresses a person suffering from depression,
and contains hints of Robert Frost's 'The Road Not Taken', and Yeats's
assertion that 'We begin to live when we have conceived life as tragedy':

> Fé mar a thit cúrsaí amach,
> is minic a bhí an bealach
> lán d'achrann, mearbhall is leonadh

agus gach tarna cor ann gan choinne,
mar cheannbhrat fite droighneach.
Ach d'ainneoin blas airní a bheith searbh
maireann neacha na samhlaíochta fén droighean.

In 'Teagmháil Fothoinn' Ó Faoláin uses the vocabulary of diving as he describes watching an ultrasound scan of a baby in the womb; he compares the child's heartbeat to the sound of a propeller underwater, and there is the lovely image of 'scamall álainn airgead éisc'. Elsewhere there are poems exploring the elusive nature of reality and of poetry. In 'Éigrit' he has the gorgeous phrase 'Maignéisiam ag dó na habhann'. In 'Cat Schrödinger' he writes: 'D'fhéadfadh an splanc sa bhosca / A bheith beo nó marbh, / Nó an dá rud araon.'

In 'Kapadokya' he vividly pictures the cave temples and underground cities of a lost civilisation, bringing to mind 'Siadsan a thochail amach na seomraí, / na tithe, na sáipéil seo'; and describes a bizarre mural of the transgender St Onophrius, 'Brat duilleog ar a t(h)óin'. 'An Cruthaitheoir' is perhaps one of the best poems in *As Gaineamh*. Here the archaeologist attempts to breathe life into 'fíricí seasca loma'; in his mind's eye, bones take on flesh, he sees animals and people hunting, the construction of palisades. But it is all 'mar chlúmh ar phuth gaoithe', like downy feathers drifting on a breath of wind. He concludes with the haunting lines:

Anois fág mar atáid, leag uait do pheann,
Ná fiafraigh an rabhadar riamh ann.

'Tromluí', a neat little poem near the end of *As Gaineamh* immediately evokes Henry Fuseli's 1781 painting *The Nightmare*. Here is the poem in its entirety:

An tusa
An taibhse
A bhí
'Na suí
Ar m'ucht
Anocht?

There's a brilliant sparseness to this poem, and it's in stark contrast to the density of 'Eachtra Siocáin', where long lines are split in two across the page. It's a challenging tour-de-force of battle and myth, referencing Cú Chulainn and Ferdia, Ragnarök, and Icarus. The telling is staccato but urgent.

There's a lot going on in *As Gaineamh* – quotes from Ezekiel, nods to William Blake and Ted Hughes, tales of life and community in Kerry, classical images. Ó Faoláin puts a lot into his poems, sometimes too much. But that is a minor criticism. Ó Faoláin is an impressive writer, not afraid to take risks with both subject matter and form. His 9/11 poem 'Leoithne ón Murascaill' is easily one of the best I've read on the subject, funny, sharp and dark in its treatment of casual racism and dehumanisation. He is a poet to be watched.

'Loving is a journey with water and with stars' wrote Neruda (translation Stephen Mitchell), and in her début collection *Crithloinnir*, Caitríona Ní Chléirchín echoes much of his romantic-erotic lexicon of stars, flowers, skies, waves, moonlight, night, sea. Her poems are delicate, airy constructions, sparse, intimate. This is a world of *amour fou*, of passion, of sensuality. It is almost a self-enclosed world, a secret world – again and again Ní Chléirchín uses the word 'rúnda', or secretive. It's worth remembering that in Irish 'rún' can mean a secret or a lover. We have 'réaltaí rúnda', and in 'Cathair rúnda', her lovers wander through an anonymous spectral city; they are 'dall' and 'bodhar', blind and deaf to all that is urban – people, cars, traffic – and see only 'féar, duilleoga, / is linnte'. She frequently uses the word 'bladhm' – a flame, a blaze, a splash of sunshine. Like the compound word 'crithloinnir' it summons the 'shivering blaze' of love.

Her best love poems are those which contain notes of tension and darkness, the sense that love might be fleeting or deceptive. In 'Nóiméad ar maidin', she watches a lover iron his shirt, smoothing out creases, wryly hinting that all may not remain blissful:

> Tá súil agam go mbeidh cúrsaí eadrainn
>   chomh réidh sin, a stór.

'Café Java' likewise speaks of 'gaoth an fhocail / ar an uisce // mar thuar ar a bhfuil / romhainn', and the word 'tuar' is one that contains a sense of dark omens, grim forebodings.

'Scáil' is, for my money, the best poem in *Crithloinnir*. It's a poem of self-doubt – 'd'imigh na focail ó mo chroí / gan cheol'. She sees her words as hollow, empty, herself as a shadow, she is 'gan guth, gan teanga'. It's a subtle play on the hackneyed slogan 'tír gan teanga, tír gan anam'. Here, language loss, or a feeling of being able to express oneself, is a personal rather than a national issue. 'Look at my shadow, there's nothing here of me', wrote Marina Tsvetaeva, and there are more than a few echoes, intentional or otherwise, of the spectral romanticism of the Russian Silver Age. *Crithloinnir* is an unashamed collection of love poems, they are clear, open, deftly lyrical. It will be interesting to see what Ní Chléirchín is capable of once she moves to new thematic territory.

Notes on Contributors

Dr Fran Brearton is Reader in English at Queen's University Belfast. She is author of *The Great War in Irish Poetry* (OUP, 2000) and *Reading Michael Longley* (Bloodaxe Books, 2006). She is currently co-editing *The Oxford Handbook of Modern Irish Poetry*.

Colm Breathnach has been published by both Coiscéim and Cló Iar-Chonnachta, and his collections include *Cantaic an Bhalbháin* (1991), *An Fearann Breac* (1992), *Scáthach* (1994), *An Fear Marbh* (1998) and *Chiaroscuro* (2006).

Liam Carson is Director of the IMRAM Irish Language Literature Festival. His memoir, *Call Mother A Lonely Field*, is published by Hag's Head Press.

Harry Clifton's *Secular Eden: Paris Notebooks* 1994-2004 (Wake Forest University Press, 2007), won the 2008 *Irish Times Poetry Now Award*. He is the current Ireland Professor of Poetry.

Sarah Collins is currently studying for the MA in Creative Writing at the University of Manchester, where she also works as a Lecturer in Communication. She is previously published in *Best of Manchester Poets*.

Tom Duddy's début collection, *The Hiding Place*, was published this year by Arlen House. He teaches Philosophy in the School of Humanities at NUI, Galway.

Lynne Edgar has been published in *The Belfast Telegraph*, the *Derry Journal*, the *Londonderry Sentinel*, *Ulla's Nib* and the online *Speech Therapy*. Her first collection of poems, *Trapeze*, will be published in the autumn by Lapwing.

Tom French's collections *Touching the Bones* (2001) and *The Fire Step* (2009) are published by Gallery Press. He edited *A Meath Anthology* (Meath County Council Library Service) in 2010, and an essay 'The Hummingbird of Athboy' appeared recently in the third *John McGahern Yearbook*.

Miriam Gamble's first collection, *The Squirrels Are Dead*, is published by Bloodaxe and won a Somerset Maugham Award in 2011. She works as a subtitler for the hard of hearing.

Matthew Geden lives in Kinsale, Co Cork where he runs Kinsale Bookshop. His publications include *Kinsale Poems, Autumn: Twenty Poems by Guillaume Apollinaire* and, most recently, *Swimming to Albania*, which was published in 2009 by Bradshaw Books.

Vona Groarke has published five collections with Gallery Press, most recently *Spindrift*, a Poetry Book Society recommendation in 2009. She teaches in the Centre for New Writing at the University of Manchester.

Daniel Hardisty's poems have previously appeared in *Poetry Ireland Review*, *Poetry London*, *The Rialto*, *New Welsh Review* and elsewhere. He is currently studying for a Creative Writing Ph.D. at Newcastle University.

Jodie Hollander, a poet and teacher originally from Milwaukee, Wisconsin, was raised in a family of classical musicians. Her poems are published in *Under the Radar*, *Poetry Salzburg*, *The Warwick Review*, *Poetry New Zealand*, the *James Dickey Review* and *Page Seventeen*. She is an accomplished tennis player, and is currently compiling her first collection.

Rae Howells studied the MA in Novel Writing at Manchester University, and was shortlisted for the Rhys Davies Short Story Prize and the Arvon International Poetry Competition, and published in the *New Welsh Review*. She is currently researching a Ph.D. at Cardiff University.

Bethan Kilfoil is from Wales and lives in Co Kildare. She works as a journalist for RTÉ. 'Silhouette' is her first published poem.

Frances-Anne King's poetry is widely published in *Acumen*, *Agenda*, *Envoi*, *The Rialto*, *Poetry Wales*, and elsewhere.

Thomas Kinsella, born in Dublin in 1928, resigned from a career in the Deptartment of Finance for a life in poetry in the USA. His translations include *The Táin* and *An Duanaire 1600-1900: Poems of the Dispossessed*, and in 1986 he edited *The New Oxford Book of Irish Verse*. His *Collected Poems* appeared in 2001 and Dedalus Press continue to publish his Peppercanister pamphlets. In 2007 Kinsella received the Freedom of Dublin city.

Jaki McCarrick writes plays, poetry and prose. Last year she won the John Lennon Poetry Prize for her poem, 'The Selkie of Dorinish'. Her story 'The Visit' won the 2010 Wasafiri New Writing Prize (Fiction) and is to appear in the forthcoming anthology of *Best British Short Stories* (Salt Publishing). She has just completed her first collection of short stories, *Badlands*.

Ted McCarthy's collection *November Wedding and Other Poems* was published by Lilliput Press in 1998. He is widely published in Ireland, the UK, Europe and the United States.

Iggy McGovern's first collection, *The King of Suburbia*, was the winner of the inaugural Glen Dimplex New Writers Award for Poetry in 2006. His second collection, *Safe House*, was published, also by Dedalus Press, in 2010.

Derek Mahon's *New Collected Poems* was published earlier this year by Gallery Press.

Mark Mullee was born in Houston, Texas. His poetry has appeared previously in *Poetry Ireland Review*.

Richard Murphy's *New Collected Poems* will be published next year by Lilliput Press. Much of his work appears in Patrick Crotty's *The Penguin Book of Irish Poetry* (2010) and in Wes Davis's *An Anthology of Modern Irish Poetry* (Belknap/Harvard, 2010). Granta Books published his memoir *The Kick* in 2002, and Gallery Press his *Collected Poems* in 2000. Since he turned 80 in 2007, he has been writing and living, for reasons of health, economy, and the kindness of people, in the highlands of Sri Lanka, formerly Ceylon, where his Irish-born father's career in the British Colonial Service stretched from 1910 to 1942.

Caitríona Ní Chléirchín is originally from Gortmoney, Emyvale in Co Monaghan. She is an Irish-language lecturer in University College Dublin and is completing a doctorate on the poetry of Nuala Ní Dhomhnaill and Biddy Jenkinson. *Crithloinnir,* her début collection of poetry, won first prize in the Oireachtas competition for new writers in 2010.
Is as Gort na Móna, Scairbh na gCaorach i gCo Mhuineacháin ó dhúchas do **Chaitríona Ní Chléirchín**. Léachtóir le Gaeilge í i gColáiste na hOllscoile Bhaile Átha Cliath agus tá sí ag críochniú dochtúireachta ar fhilíocht Nuala Ní Dhomhnaill agus Biddy Jenkinson faoi láthair. Bhuaigh a cnuasach filíochta *Crithloinnir* an chéad duais san Oireachtas i gComórtas na Scríbhneoirí Úra 2010.

Kate Noakes is a Welsh academician. Her most recent collection is *The Wall Menders* (Two Rivers Press, 2009). She won the Owen Barfield Prize in 2009 and is a regular performer at readings and festivals in the UK. She blogs at **www.boomslangpoetry.blogspot.com**

D Nurkse is the author of nine books of poetry, most recently *The Border Kingdom*. He received a 2009 Literature Award from the American Academy of Arts and Letters.

Proinsias Ó Drisceoil is the author of *Ar Scaradh Gabhail: An Fhéiniúlacht in Cín Lae Amhlaoibh Uí Shúilleabháin* (Clóchomhar, 2000) and *Seán Ó Dálaigh: Éigse agus Iomarbhá* (Cork University Press, 2007), as well as many essays on Gaelic literature.

James Owens lives in New Carlisle, Indiana. Two books of his poems have been published: *An Hour is the Doorway* (Black Lawrence Press) and *Frost Lights a Thin Flame* (Mayapple Press). His poems, reviews, translations and photographs have appeared widely in literary journals, including recent or upcoming publications in *The Cortland Review, The Cresset*, and *The Chaffey Review*.

Paul Perry's most recent books include *108 Moons: The Selected Poems of Jurga Ivanauskaitė* (The Workshop Press, 2010) and *The Last Falcon and Small Ordinance* (Dedalus Press, 2010). He is editor of *Beyond the Workshop*, forthcoming from Kingston University Press.

Thomas Dillon Redshaw is a former editor of *Éire-Ireland* and *New Hibernia Review*. He is also the editor of *Well Dreams: Essays on John Montague* (Creighton University Press, 2004).

Denis Rigal, born in 1938, lives in Brest (Finistère). His most recent collection, *Aval*, appeared from Gallimard in 2006.

Gabriel Rosenstock's most recent publications are the children's books *Sa Tóir ar an Yeití* (Cló Mhaigh Eo) and his retellings of ancient and medieval Indian tales, *Birbal* (Cló Iar-Chonnachta). He is represented in *Best European Fiction* 2012 (Dalkey Archive Press).

Gerard Smyth's poetry has appeared widely in publications in Ireland, Britain and America, as well as in translation. His work also features regularly on Irish radio. He is the author of seven collections, the most recent of which is *The Fullness of Time: New and Selected Poems* (Dedalus Press, 2010). He is a member of Aosdána.

Rabindranath Tagore (1861–1941), poet, novelist, playwright, short story writer, song writer and painter, was the first Asian Nobel Laureate. *Stray Birds* (1916), from which selections are included in this issue, was written in Bengali after his visit to Japan.

Marina Tsvetaeva (1892-1941) was the last of Russia's acclaimed quartet of twentieth-century poets (with Mandelstam, Pastenak and Akhmatova) to be 'discovered' in the West. Despite her long and tragic exile in both Paris and Prague she never lost her roots in Russia and the tradition of Russian poetry. Ostracised on her return to Russia and living in severe circumstances, she took her life in 1941.

Grace Wells's début collection, *When God Has Been Called Away to Greater Things* (Dedalus Press) won the 2011 Rupert and Eithne Strong Best First Collection Award and was short-listed for the London Fringe Festival New Poetry Award. She reviews Irish poetry for the University of Chicago's online literary journal, *Contrary*, and for *The Stinging Fly*.

John White is a graduate of the Oxford Masters Degree in Creative Writing. His work has appeared in *Oxford Poets* 2007 (edited by Bernard O'Donoghue and David Constantine) and in *Agenda* and *Oxford* magazines, and in 2010 he was a winner in the Parallel UniVerse Poetry Competition, for poems on a scientific or medical theme.

Christopher Whyte's third Gaelic collection *Dealbh Athar* was published by Coiscéim in 2009, with facing translations by Gréagóir Ó Dúill. Poets he has translated into English include Rainer Maria Rilke, Pier Paolo Pasolini, Gabriel Ferrater and Dezső Tandori. He is author of the monograph *Modern Scottish Poetry* (Edinburgh University Press, 2004) and joint editor of the new collected poems of Sorley MacLean, *Caoir Gheal Leumraich / A White Leaping Flame* (Birlinn and Carcanet, 2011).

Howard Wright's début collection, *King and Country*, was published last year by Blackstaff Press, and earlier this year Templar Press published his pamphlet, *Blue Murder*. Recent poems have appeared in *Iota*, *Cyphers* and *The Frogmore Papers*.

Jane Yeh's first collection, *Marabou*, was shortlisted for the Whitbread, Forward, and Jerwood Aldeburgh Poetry Prizes. Her next book, *The Ninjas*, will be published by Carcanet in 2012.